MAGIC
AND
MYSTERIES
OF
ANCIENT
EGYPT

MAGIC
AND
MYSTERIES
OF
ANCIENT
EGYPT

JAMES BENNETT AND
VIVIANNE CROWLEY

Sterling Publishing Co., Inc.
New York

Library of Congress Cataloging-in-Publication Data Available

10 9 8 7 6 5 4 3 2 1

Published·in 2001 by Sterling Publishing Company, Inc.

387 Park Avenue South, New York, N.Y. 10016

© 2001 Godsfield Press

Text © 2001 James Bennett and Vivianne Crowley

Distributed in Canada by Sterling Publishing

c/o Canadian Manda Group, One Atlantic Avenue, Suite 105

Toronto, Ontario, Canada M6K 3E7

Distributed in Australia by Capricorn Link (Australia) Pty Ltd

P O. Box 6651, Baulkham Hills, Business Centre, NSW 2153, Australia

Printed and bound in China

Sterling ISBN 0-8069-2650-3

Contents

Introduction   6

Chapter 1 Egypt and the Egyptians   10

Chapter 2 Religion in Ancient Egypt   28

Chapter 3 Magic and Amulets   42

Chapter 4 Astrology and Time   54

Chapter 5 Language and Hieroglyphs   68

Chapter 6 Sex and Love Magic   80

Chapter 7 Divination and Dreams   88

Chapter 8 Figures and Images in Egyptian Magic   100

Chapter 9 Health and Healing   108

Chapter 10 Learning More   124

Glossary   126

Index   128

Introduction

The Wonder of Egypt

Of all the civilizations of the ancient world, Egypt is the one that holds the greatest fascination. If you fly over Egypt today, you will see a unique land. Stretching either side of the waters of the mighty everflowing River Nile is a band of green that stops abruptly five or ten miles each side of the river. Beyond this lies barren inhospitable desert. To the Egyptians, the Nile was the bringer of life, and they worshiped it as a god. Egyptian culture was extraordinarily sophisticated and both arts and sciences flourished within it. The Egyptians had a knowledge of medicine, anatomy, and engineering unsurpassed in the ancient world, and their pyramids, temples, and tombs still remain wonders today.

The kingdom of Egypt survived for over three thousand years, from around 3150 BCE to 30 BCE, when Queen Cleopatra VII was overthrown by the Romans. The fact that the world view of this civilization could be sustained over several thousand years with little outward change in language, religion, or social order is unique. Even when it was under periods of Libyan, Nubian, Persian, Greek, and Roman rule, the Egyptian lifestyle was held in high esteem and the invader adopted Egyptian customs and spiritual beliefs, such as embalming of the dead, medical treatments, and dress codes.

The Egyptians had an extremely ordered culture that was based on a pattern of natural and ritual events. It was every Egyptian's strongest desire that artistic conventions, political institutions, human behavior, attitudes, morality, and even language itself remained steadfast and predictable. This attitude meant that great things were achieved. With the hieroglyph, the Egyptians perfected the most beautiful writing in the world; their walls were painted with glorious images of deities and nature; the arts of civilization, such as dance and music, were honed to perfection in Egyptian temples and homes; and the images they created of their deities still resonate with power and meaning millennia after they were first painted and carved in stone. Above all, the Egyptians understood the sciences of mind and spirit. Their understanding of spiritual realms, the levels of consciousness achievable by the human mind, and of those hidden powers of the mind that we call psychic and magical, was unsurpassed. It is for this reason that Egypt and its fascinating culture continues to interest and enthrall us today.

The genius of the Egyptians was that they created deities that are archetypal, such as Isis. The beautiful symmetry of their images inspires us and speaks to the unconscious in a way that other deities do not. Egypt might be known simply as the land of the pyramids to many people, but these architectural relics are only a small part of the fascinating whole.

About this Book

In *Magic and Mysteries of Ancient Egypt*, we will take you on a journey into the magical world of the Ancient Egyptians. Whether you have visited Egypt or are planning to, or whether such a trip must remain for the present a dream, this book will allow you to understand the magical world view that underpinned the civilization of Egypt. Religion, mysticism, and magic were threads that ran through every aspect of Ancient Egyptian life. In this book we describe the land of Egypt, its people, the deities they worshiped, their myths, and religion. You will also learn how the Ancient Egyptians used their psychic and magical powers to help them in everyday life; we describe Egyptian incantations and spells and how you can harness your own magical energy using the symbolism of Egypt. You will see that such inner powers can allow us to utilize our creativity and make positive changes within our lives.

Time and Space

The ancients believed that the world and all objects were full of energy. They understood this intuitively but did not have the technology to prove it. Quantum physics has since demonstrated that many ideas once considered "magical" are theoretically possible, indeed even probable. Phenomena such as telepathy, which most people have experienced occasionally and a few people experience frequently, were dismissed by early 20th-century science.

With our new understanding of time and space, we know that such phenomena can occur. Different times can coexist and events that are separated in space can influence one another. Science has shown us that every physical thing is an interacting synthesis of energy particles. Studies of the cosmic microwave background of the universe show that space is full of what is known as "dark energy." We do not yet know how to harness this energy, but one day we will.

Experience not Belief

The 21st century is the era of the experiential. We do not ask you to believe that a meditation to Isis will change your inner state of being, but we suggest that you try it and see. Most of the exercises in this book are "magical" in the sense that the effect they have on our lives can be magical. Some exercises go a step beyond this. The healing exercise in Chapter 9 (*pp. 122–3*) is a communication between your mind and the person to whom you are directing the healing. It is a manifestation of positive thought and love toward another. This shows you that your inner state of being can influence someone else's, and requires a complex model of human psychology that implies our psyches are not completely separate from one another. You do not need to believe this, but you can try the exercise to see if it works. Of course, this idea has wider implications. If we are connected to one another then it is important that we seek to manifest positive energies in our own psyches. These will influence the group psyche of our species; by working with others, each of us has something to contribute to help the evolution of humankind.

A Spirituality for the 21st Century

In studying Ancient Egypt, we grow closer to the ancients whose wisdom preceded us and who left us a rich spiritual inheritance from which we can draw. The past is important because it can hold up a mirror to our contemporary world and can give us insights into how we live our lives in the present. Ancient Egypt speaks in a powerful voice that transcends boundaries of race, language, and nation. The archetypal images of Egyptian goddesses and gods are so potent that they are worshiped all over the world by people who have no physical kinship with Egypt but feel a deep spiritual link with that ancient civilization. One leading organization in this endeavor is the Fellowship of Isis. Based in Ireland, this group is active in reviving goddess spirituality all over the world, for, although Egyptian spirituality is an African tradition, people of European, African, and Asian descent, and many others, are drawn to the worship of the goddess Isis.

We are not looking with nostalgia for wisdom from the past but are seeking to move forward into a new and evolving form of spirituality. Isis is the goddess of the new eon. She redresses the balance of two thousand years of patriarchal dogma and the debasement of the feminine. She is all-nurturing, healing, and loving. She is our mother, our sister, our lover, ourselves. Her protection reaches out from the past to shield our future.

RIGHT

A felucca sailing on the River Nile at Aswan. Feluccas are able to sail in the slightest breeze. Their design has remained unchanged for thousands of years.

1

Egypt and the Egyptians

The Nile is unique among the rivers of the world because it flows from south to north—from central Africa to the Mediterranean Sea. The land stretching from the modern city of Aswan to modern Cairo was known as Upper Egypt, while Lower Egypt extended from Cairo to the Nile Delta, the Faiyum, and the Mediterranean Sea.

To the north, the Nile branches into smaller rivers and streams that fan out across the fertile Faiyum delta. This is the khemet, *or "black land," the name the Egyptians gave to their country. You need only grab a handful of this rich, black, silty soil to understand the Egyptians' love of their land.*

Like many people in the ancient world, the Egyptians believed that the east and the rising sun were associated with birth, and the west and the setting sun with death. Since agricultural land was too valuable for cemeteries, the land of the desert ridge of the western bank of the Nile was ideal for monuments to the dead.

LEFT
The Nile Delta is one of the landmarks that can be seen from space easily. This demonstrates its sheer size and importance to the land that is Egypt today.

Narmer, Lord of the Two Lands

The Ancient Egyptians kept the political and cultural distinction between Upper and Lower Egypt throughout their 3,000-year history. Originally, they were two separate cultural and political entities, until Menes (which may have been another name for the pharaoh Narmer) became the first great Egyptian king. He was born in Hierakonpolis in southern Egypt and he united the two kingdoms through a combination of warfare and diplomacy. Narmer was given the title Neb Tawy, Lord of the Two Lands, and it was from this time that the Egyptian pharaohs came to wear a double crown—the inner white crown of Upper Egypt with the red crown of Lower Egypt surrounding it. Lord of the Two Lands was one of the most important of all the royal titles.

Farming Begins

The early Egyptians built small villages on the edge of the floodplain or on top of the natural banks and raised ground that the floods never reached. They began to rely increasingly upon their domesticated animals and agriculture to feed a growing community. One of the most important prerequisites for the growth of civilization is the creation of a predictable food supply and the administrative structure to store and distribute it. In Egypt the main staple for life was barley and wheat.

ABOVE
An 18th dynasty tomb painting of Nebamum and his family hunting wild birds, British Museum. Note the cat which is used to fetch birds injured by the throw stick.

LEFT
Wheat was a mainstay of the Egyptian economy, giving Egypt the nickname "the breadbasket of the world."

ABOVE
*Grain provided bread and another
mainstay of the Egyptian diet—beer.*

Grain was the single most important commodity and was used as currency. Grain was used in trade for a wide array of basic and luxury items and, of course, grain was brewed into beer—another staple. One of the reasons that the Romans invaded Egypt was because of its grain. Some of Egypt's greatest monuments were vast storehouses for tons of cereal grain. Cereal growing was made possible for the Ancient Egyptians because the Nile flooded on a regular basis. Until the Aswan Dam was constructed in the 1960s, the dry desert air meant that clouds did not form easily over Upper Egypt and there was very little rainfall. Instead, the Ancient Egyptians benefited from what is called flood basin agriculture. Each summer, melted snow from the African mountains far to the south and annual rainfall in central Africa fed the numerous tributaries of the Nile until, when

RIGHT
A carved palette, c. 3500 BCE, shows King Narmer, thought to be the first king of the unified states of Upper and Lower Egypt, defeating his enemies.

it reached Egypt, the river burst its banks and flooded the land. The flood brought water and fresh silt to fertilize the soil. Now that the Aswan Dam has been built, modern Egypt relies on artificial fertilizer.

Egyptian Ingenuity
The flood would have been of little use without the sophisticated civil engineering techniques that were developed successfully by the Egyptians. Not a drop of water was wasted. The floodwater was expertly directed into irrigation channels and subsidiary ditches that took water to every single field. No further watering was needed.

Egyptian Society

Architecture often reflects a society's view of itself. One of the symbols we associate most strongly with Ancient Egypt is the pyramid. Egyptian society was a social pyramid with the pharaoh standing at its pinnacle. Below him were the remaining members of the royal family, most importantly the queen and the first-born prince. Below them were the nobility, a hereditary line of significant leaders in their own local areas of Egypt. A senior noble family with close ties to the throne would provide a vizier or chief administrative officer to the pharaoh. He would act much as a prime minister does today to a monarch. Next level down would be the professional classes— the doctors, sculptors, business people, and minor members of the civil service. Supporting the remainder of the pyramid, and providing its firm base, were the farmers and workers who produced the essential food supplies that fed the population.

The Egyptian Royal Family

The pharaoh was considered to be divine. In theory, he held absolute and unquestioning authority over his people, especially in the earlier periods of Egyptian history when he was considered to be a god on earth. By the time of the New Kingdom (1567–1320 BCE), when Tutankhamun was in power, a new secular political consensus had evolved where the pharaoh ruled by divine authority rather than by divine manifestation. Certainly the pharaoh's word was law. He was expected to provide national defense and internal security. He was the direct link with the divine, so the success or failure of climate and crops was his responsibility. As head of the administration, he was responsible for ensuring that all the departments under his watchful eye were functioning properly. As chief justice, his wisdom and decision-making skills in disputes were absolute.

The queens of Egypt enjoyed their own power and prestige and were frequently related to the pharaoh through close kinship. Principal queens would have had their own estates to manage. Frequently, they would live on these estates and raise their children while the pharaoh saw to the affairs of state. The political role of the queen seemed to grow increasingly more important throughout Egyptian history and this

RIGHT
Saqqara, the Step Pyramid of King Zoser. This pyramid is about 4,600 years old.

culminated in a number of powerful queens in the New Kingdom. Although the queen could always act as regent while her child was still in infancy, it was expected that she would hand over formal power at an appointed time. One queen, Hatshepsut, of the 18th Egyptian dynasty, assumed all the titles and functions of pharaoh and did not relinquish power until her death. Her son, who became Tutmosis III, was appointed general of the army and was sent on years of foreign campaigns. Another later queen in the same dynasty, Queen Nefertiti, ran the affairs of state while her visionary husband, Akhenaten, meditated upon his god.

In addition to his secular roles, the pharaoh was considered the incarnation of Amun, chief of the gods, who was symbolized by the powerful, fertile, and dangerous wild desert bull. The pharaoh acted as chief priest of Amun and the queen was the chief priestess. The close association between the pharaoh and the god Amun made the cult and priesthood of Amun one of the most economically powerful independent institutions in the state. Despite their role as chief priest, keeping a close check on the political machinations of the Amun priests was a major problem for many of Egypt's pharaohs.

Childbirth

With Egypt's high birthrate, midwives were in high demand. They were in charge of caring for the mother throughout pregnancy and delivering the baby. Before the birth, the woman would move into a specially prepared tent, away from the main house. After the baby was born, the umbilical cord was not cut until the baby had been cleansed and bathed and the placenta had appeared. The infant's afterbirth was dried and kept for magical purposes, and it always accompanied an individual to the grave.

The Egyptians classified giving birth into three types. The first was the most desirable and was called *hotep*, or strong birth: this was swift and effortless. The second type was *bened* birth, which had a complicated or potentially dangerous labor. The third type was *wedef* birth, one that becomes long and protracted. These categories indicated the varying levels of health risk to the mother and baby, rather than the degree of pain. After giving birth, woman underwent a period of 14 days' postnatal cleansing.

Contraception

Although children were badly wanted, for the sake of the mother's health and for practical reasons, parents tried to space out pregnancies. Several instructions survive for creating homemade contraceptives, the most usual being lint soaked in various substances, which could be inserted into the vagina. The Kahun Papyrus describes the use of honey as a spermicide; this may have been effective because of its osmotic effect. Breastfeeding also helped reduce the likelihood of conceiving again too quickly.

LEFT
A doting father with his three children, who have the forelock and partially shaved heads of youth. Painting in the tomb of Inherkha, Deir El Medineh, West Thebes, 18th dynasty.

LEFT
*The goddess Isis, devoted wife, mother,
and mistress of magic, was venerated in Egypt
and beyond for thousands of years.
Here, Isis is suckling her son Horus.*

Childhood

Egyptian inheritance custom meant that it was sons who were responsible for providing the funeral rites for parents, so the birth of male children was important to Egyptian families. However, daughters were valued much more highly in Egyptian society than in other contemporary cultures and women had greater social freedom. The best education was reserved for the royal family and the nobility, whose children received private instruction in the palace: girls learned music, singing, dancing, and the arts; boys were apprenticed into a trade that could serve the state. For the majority of children who did not go to school, responsibilities began early. Young boys and girls were expected to contribute as soon as possible to the family income. Among the many chores of an Egyptian child were fetching and carrying, childcare, threshing grain, herding goats, household chores, or making bread.

From Child to Adult

Children are obvious in Egyptian art, not only because they are sculpted on a smaller scale but also because of the forelock of youth that they all have. Egyptian children had shaven heads except for a forelock of hair that was left on the side of the head. This was elaborately beaded and braided and allowed to grow long. Boys' and girls' puberty was celebrated by an initiation ritual into adulthood where the forelock was ritually cut. From that point on, the adolescent adopted an adult hairstyle. Boys were also circumcised at puberty, a practice still found in some Muslim and African countries. The tomb of Ankhmahor at Saqqara, dated to the 6th dynasty, shows a wall carving of two boys being circumcised. One is having a pain-killing unguent applied, while the other appears to be distressed.

Like Father, Like Son

Boys were expected to follow in their father's footsteps and take over his job when he retired. For an important position, such as the vizier or a chief adviser to the pharaoh, a boy would have undergone rigorous training in reading, writing, geography, mathematics, and administration. Other important posts, such as chief scribe and chief accountant of the treasury, were filled by men educated in special schools set up by administrative departments. These offered the best education available. One textbook, called the Papyrus Anastasi 5, describes a curriculum of training for pupils planning on entering politics, the diplomatic service, or the army. The subjects included the geography of Asia, arithmetic sums in a military context, and foreign languages. The education of middle-class Egyptian children was similar but more narrowly focused than that received by nobles.

Middle-class children who were expected to enter specific professions would have a period of apprenticeship not unlike that found in many parts of the world today. Their knowledge of reading, writing, and mathematics would be rudimentary and limited to what they needed to know. Apprenticeship usually started at 12 to 14 years of age and lasted for three years. The first two years were unpaid, while the apprentice was learning the trade, and the third year was salaried. An apprenticeship was primarily a middle-class prerogative for sculptors, artists, metalworkers, jewelers, weavers, and potters. However, Egypt had a class system rather than a caste system. Promising students from even the lowest ranks of Egyptian society could, through diligence and application, work their way into the highest ranks of the professions to reach important administrative positions.

Play

Egyptian childhood was not totally dominated by work and education. Toys are among the most interesting kinds of artifacts left behind by any culture; indeed, there are certain types of toys and games that seem to be fairly universal. It was not until the mechanical age in the 19th century that toys became

LEFT
A tomb painting showing the paramilitary training of young men. They are wrestling, doing gymnastics, and fighting with sticks. From the tomb of Nomarch Khnum-hotep, Middle Kingdom.

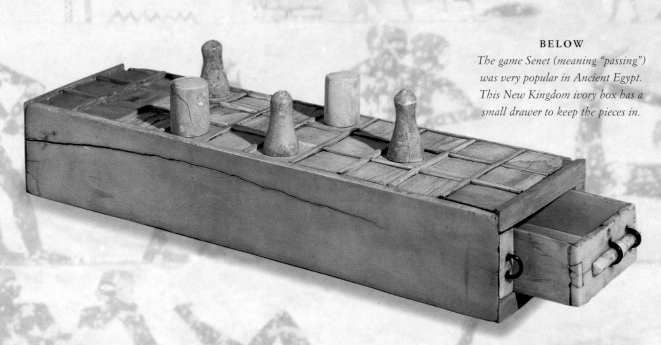

BELOW
The game Senet (meaning "passing")
was very popular in Ancient Egypt.
This New Kingdom ivory box has a
small drawer to keep the pieces in.

so diverse and complicated. Dolls, for instance, have been made since the earliest times. Children who died were buried with their favorite toys so that they would be with them in the afterlife. One child's tomb at the site of Hawara, dating from the 12th dynasty, is of a little girl called Sitrennut. Her favorite wooden doll with moveable arms was buried with her, as was her small wooden child's bed. Other dolls have been found in tombs with complete sets of clothes.

There are many types of toys and games from Ancient Egypt that children still play with today. A good example is the simple ball. Numerous balls made from wood or pieces of leather, stuffed and stitched together, were discovered in the Middle Kingdom town of Kahun. One of the balls was repaired many times, so it must have been a prized possession. In the ancient world, portable personal possessions were relatively rare and expensive. If people broke something, they did not discard it and buy a new one, as these items had great personal value. Clothes, shoes, tools, utensils, furniture, and toys were all repaired and reused.

From tomb paintings we can see many types of ball games. Balls were used for juggling; another painting shows four girls standing foursquare, clapping their hands while they catch and throw a ball that is passed round the group. Sport and physical fitness were very important to the Ancient Egyptians. Competitive games with established rules included archery, wrestling, foot races, chariot races, spear throwing, acrobatics, arm wrestling, and gymnastics. Even the pharaoh is depicted at Luxor playing a curious game involving a stick and a ball, possibly similar to the English game of cricket.

What did the Ancient Egyptians look like?

The people of Egypt were a mixture of the indigenous African inhabitants of the Nile region and the Semitic people who migrated into Egypt from the eastern Mediterranean and Middle East. Ancient Egyptian tomb paintings show attractive, brown-skinned people with black hair. The average Ancient Egyptian was shorter than the inhabitants of Egypt today. Men had an average height of 5 ft. 2 in., with women averaging 4 ft. 10 in. Skin color and facial features would have been darker and more African in appearance in the south than in the north near the Mediterranean Sea, where people had intermarried

with eastern Mediterranean peoples such as Greeks and Syrians. Some Egyptians did suffer from the modern Western condition of obesity but it was found only among the rich, who did not have to engage in physical work. Most of the population would have been slightly built but sinewy and finely muscled because of the exercise involved in stone-masonry, farming, or laboring. The attractive physical appearance of the Egyptians that can be seen from wall paintings was due partly to artistic convention and partly to the age of the population. Mortality rates were high. Around half of the three-million-strong population would die by the age of 35. As in developing countries today, the population was sustained by a high birth rate.

Diet

Health and physical beauty are the result of a good diet that includes plenty of variety and the correct balance of proteins, carbohydrates, fats, vitamins, and minerals. Many Ancient Egyptians had a diet that was almost as varied as our own. Emmer wheat and barley were mainstays of the Egyptian diet and were used to make bread and beer, two important staples. Vegetables, including cabbage, chickpeas, lettuce, cucumber, lentils, onions, peas, radishes,

LEFT

The Ancient Egyptians were a beautiful, graceful people. These female musicians are playing the flute, harp, and lute. A painting from the Theban tomb of the scribe Nakht, 18th dynasty.

beans, garlic, leeks, and celery, were grown as a large-scale industry and in countless small garden plots attached to private homes. Cooking oil could be produced from vegetables. A wide variety of fruits and nuts were available, including apples, carob, dates, doum palm, figs, grapes, olives, damsons, apricots, plums, bananas, pomegranates, almonds, sesame seeds, and several varieties of melons. Fish and wild fowl, such as ducks and geese, supplied white meat. Dairy products were produced from cattle and goats. A wide variety of subtle flavors came from an array of spices that were to become highly prized in the Western world in later periods of history, including aniseed, chervil, cinnamon, cilantro, dill, licorice, fenugreek, bay, basil, thyme, rosemary, safflower, parsley, mustard, oregano, cumin, cardamom, mint, sage, and marjoram, and are still valued today.

A good diet usually means a longer, healthier life. However, despite the great variety of foods that was available in Ancient Egypt, the full range may have been accessible only to those who were wealthier than the average peasant. Like modern society, the rich of Ancient Egypt could afford to buy better food and tended to live longer. One study of Late Period burials at Abusir found the average age of death for peasant farmers to be 20 years for men and 17 years for women. Infectious diseases were major hazards. Typhoid fever, diphtheria, typhus, influenza, plague, and a host of other diseases could spread rapidly throughout the population.

Life after Death

Ancient Egypt is most famous for its spectacular tombs, such as the pyramids at Giza and the tombs of the Valley of the Kings and Valley of the Queens on the west bank of the Nile, opposite modern-day Luxor. Egyptian attempts to preserve the body were some of the most extreme to be found in any civilization. So strong was the belief in the afterlife that a lot of money was spent on embalming, coffins, sarcophagi, and the tombs themselves.

The Ancient Egyptians' preoccupation with death, the afterlife, and tomb building becomes more understandable once we know that death could come so unexpectedly and that few people could hope to survive to old age. Infants were particularly vulnerable to diseases such as gastroenteritis. Other causes of infant death were potentially fatal hazards such as scorpion stings and snake bites. Infant mortality was around 20–25 per cent: up to one in every four children would die during infancy.

The Egyptians believed that the artifacts buried with the body could be used when the person awoke in the afterlife, so royalty and the wealthy filled their tombs with furniture, clothing, gold jewelry, and every possible comfort they might need in their next stage of existence. In their desire to preserve the body uncorrupted, the Egyptians developed elaborate embalming techniques to turn the corpse into a bandage-covered mummy. The Egyptians expected the afterlife to be like this one, only better. Tomb paintings show people fishing, fowling, partying, working, and sitting with their families. Small clay models of bakers, brewers, and numerous other professionals ensured that their products would be enjoyed as well. Families were keen to be reunited in the afterlife. Several family members would be buried in different chambers in the same tomb and, if they had servants, the servants would also be buried in the same tomb or nearby.

LEFT

The vestibule of the Tomb of Nefertari, Valley of the Queens, Luxor. Nefertari was the wife of Rameses II. She was one of the most famous of Egypt's queens and was venerated as a goddess.

The Blessing of a Long Life

While the poorer died younger, the middle classes could expect an extra ten years. Many of the wealthy would hope to reach the ripe old age of 50. Pharaohs were known to reach more than 80 years of age and some lived even longer: Pepi II reigned for 94 years. Of course, he, like other pharaohs, had access to the best doctors, diet, and lifestyle. More importantly, the pharaohs and their families lived away from the vast bulk of the population. They rarely came into contact with infectious diseases. With few people living to old age, the Egyptians esteemed their elderly and treated them with respect and veneration. They were valued for their experience and wisdom, and reaching old age was a sign of being especially blessed by the gods.

Those who were favored by the gods were said to be able to live to the age of 100 or even 110, a figure that is mentioned 27 times in texts from the Old Kingdom (2686–2181 BCE). An Egyptian living during the time of the Ptolemy dynasty of pharaohs, which lasted from Ptolemy I Soter (305 BCE) to the famous Cleopatra VII (51–30 BCE), wrote that we spend ten years as a child before we understand death and life, we then spend another ten years acquiring the instruction that enables us to live. We spend our twenties earning and gaining the possessions we need to live. We spend another ten years up to "old age" (midlife in our terms) when our hearts become our counselors. The remaining 60 years, from 40 to 100, are the whole life that the god Thoth, the ibis-headed recorder of our deeds in the halls of judgment, has assigned to the righteous. We can live long if we are aware of our lucky and unlucky days and we live in accord with divine balance. An inscription frequently found on the coffins of Ancient Egyptian nobles reads: "He who understands life will live to a hundred and ten."

LEFT
Both men and women wore jewelry to enhance their appearance. This necklace with gold pendants was made between 945–730 BCE and is now in the Egyptian Museum, Cairo.

Attuning to Ancient Egypt

Reading about Ancient Egypt is one way to bring its magic and mystical powers into your life, but this book also contains exercises to help you begin to attune to Egypt's symbolism, energies, and magical and spiritual powers.

Creating your own Egyptian Art

Egyptian culture is renowned for its very beautiful artifacts. Furniture, jewelry, and wall paintings all have an everlasting appeal. Every few years, there is a revival of interest in Egyptian artifacts and many homes all over the world are adorned with statues of Egyptian deities and papyrus paintings of scenes of Egyptian life that have been copied from tomb paintings. Many of these scenes also show Egyptian deities. Creating your own Egyptian artwork is remarkably easy. The Egyptian artist did not work alone but was an artisan who was part of a team that worked together to design, paint, and complete a wall painting. The techniques used were designed to make the work as easy as possible. A good way to begin to attune yourself to Ancient Egypt is to make your own painting of an Egyptian deity.

The most powerful Egyptian symbols are its goddesses and gods. Creating sacred images has a strong effect on the psyche. The images used by Egyptian priests and priestesses have a power and

resonance that still speak to us today. Here is an opportunity for you to create your first Egyptian artwork, an image of the goddess Isis. Isis is known in Egyptian mythology as a mistress of magic. Creating an Isis image with your own hands will allow you to begin to attune to Isis in your own life.

Preparation
Allow two hours for this exercise. The paper that you choose should be a light color so that it is easy to paint; a buff color that is similar to the color of dried

LEFT
A 13th-century BCE wall painting from the tomb of Sennedjem, Deir El Medineh, Western Thebes, showing a sacred scarab beetle carrying a gold necklace in his mouth. The scarab was a symbol of rebirth.

papyrus or white would be suitable. Some office suppliers and art shops sell parchment-type paper that would be a good background to your picture.

Because the Egyptians used only a limited range of colors, red, blue, yellow, white, and black paints should be enough for this project; you can mix most of the colors you are likely to require from these selected shades. You can add any defining lines with your black or gold pen later.

Egyptian Figure Drawing
Egyptian depictions of the human form are highly stylized. They also depict an idealized view of their subject. The men are always young and virile, the women lithe and beautiful. This was often the artist flattering the patron! Designs were based on a grid, 9 equal squares in width and 18 in height. The knee was at the sixth square from the bottom, the bottom of the hip at the ninth, and the neck at the sixteenth.

Parts of the body were drawn in such a way as to show their most characteristic feature. The face was shown in profile but with the eye full on to show the pupil, iris, and eyebrow. Shoulders were shown facing forward but with the trunk at a three-quarter angle. Like the head, the lower part of the body—feet, legs, knees, and buttocks—is shown in profile: the arch of the foot is always shown. Early paintings do not show all five toes but these begin to appear from the New Kingdom (c. 1400 BCE) onward.

Making an Image of Isis

Here we have prepared a drawing of the Egyptian goddess Isis with a grid superimposed. If you place your piece of paper in the center of the page, it will leave a border around the picture that you can use later for framing if you wish.

To make a copy, draw the faintest grid that you can, with 18 approximately ½-in squares along the vertical and 9 along the horizontal. Now copy each square of the Isis drawing onto your grid.

You should find it easy to copy the drawing using the grid system, if you just work square by square. If at this point the non-artist in you is panicking, there is another solution. For this, you will need some tracing paper, available from a toy or art shop. Simply trace the Isis picture and then copy it in one of two ways. You can place the tracing on your paper and draw over the top of the traced lines, pressing down hard the whole time. This will leave an indentation on your paper that you can then draw over. Alternatively, use a soft pencil to make the tracing and use the old childhood trick of turning the paper over and rubbing a pencil over the back of the lines you have drawn. The image will appear on your paper as a reverse of the original.

Now you can paint the image that you have drawn. In Egyptian art the hair is always black and the eyes brown, but skin color varies. Men were usually depicted with reddish-brown skin but women often had yellow skin, to indicate that they spent less time outside in the hot Egyptian sun. These skin colors were artistic conventions. Ancient Egyptians were a mixture of African and Arab peoples and their skin tone varied from light gold to black. You can follow the artistic convention, or you may prefer to paint Isis with the same skin color as your own, whatever you feel is right for this personal drawing that you are creating. Most Egyptian clothing was made from linen, which is off-white but could be dyed using vegetable and mineral dyes. Jewelry was made of gold and often contained lapis lazuli, which is a deep rich blue. You can choose other colors based on your personal preferences.

Finishing your Image

Finish your painting by taking a fine pen and outlining the main features of your drawing, to disguise any blurred edges. You might like to frame the picture. Place the picture somewhere where you can see it often. Your painting may not be the most beautiful artwork in the world, or maybe it is to you (and that is most important), but in any case, it will be a more powerful object for you than something bought from a store. Images that we have worked on ourselves have links to our unconscious psyches, the source of our hidden potential.

Now you have an image of Isis you might like to use your own words to ask her for a blessing from time to time, perhaps in the morning, before you go to bed, or whenever you need assistance.

RIGHT

The goddess Isis as Queen of Heaven—a space-age goddess to bring humanity forward to a new level of spirituality for the 21st century.

2

Religion in Ancient Egypt

To the Ancient Egyptians, the universe was a place of order and harmony. This was maintained by the power of Maat. Maat is both an abstract concept and a goddess of great power and majesty. She is order, justice, balance, cosmic harmony, and the inner voice of conscience that resides in the human heart.

After death the heart would be weighed on a set of scales, counterbalanced by a feather, the symbol of Maat. If the heart was filled with good deeds, the balance would not be tipped. If the heart was full of wickedness, the scales would swing. A monstrous beast, the devourer of souls, awaited the unworthy.

Priests and priestesses were responsible for saying the prayers and incantations that would manifest the power of their deity upon earth. To be pure of heart, they followed a strict code of ethics. They also had to be pure of body, and special cisterns or pools were provided where priests and priestesses would ritually bathe.

LEFT
The god Osiris judged the dead to determine their fate in the afterlife.
He was assisted by Maat, goddess of order, justice, truth, and ethics, shown
here with an ostrich feather on her head. From the Book of the Dead.

Deities and their Symbols

Egyptian religion appears to have a bewildering array of part-human, part-animal deities with long and exotic names. It is the religion of syncretism, where symbols of animals or objects are superimposed upon the human form to represent the divine quality of that symbol in the world of matter. The symbols associated with different deities were not arbitrary— behind the complexity is a symbolic logic.

Our ancestors everywhere were fascinated by the animal world around them. Animals exhibit certain important behavioral characteristics that our ancestors projected onto the divine. The fiercest creatures— the lioness and hippopotamus, for example—are protective mothers, so the Egyptians saw them as the most appropriate goddesses to invoke to protect women during childbirth. Cows were observed to

RIGHT
A green basalt statue of Thoth in the form of an ape. The intelligence of the ape made it an appropriate symbol for a god of learning.

give birth easily, so childbirth itself was presided over by the gentle goddess Hathor, who is depicted with a cow's head. Baboons resemble human beings and are highly intelligent. Their superior reasoning ability made the Egyptians choose them as a manifestation of the god of learning, Thoth.

Egyptian symbolic logic also extended to objects. An important feature in Egyptian architecture is the pillar. The human backbone was seen as the pillar that holds up the human body, in the same way that pillars hold up the enormous weight of a building. A symbolic pillar called the Djed column was venerated as the backbone of the god Osiris, a symbol of his strength, endurance, and power. The Djed column is also associated with the *shwnwt*, the twin pillars that the Egyptians thought held up the sky.

LEFT
Relief on a capital of the face of Hathor, with her characteristic cow ears. From the Temple of Hathor, Denderah, 116–107 BCE.

New Deities from Old

Although the Ancient Egyptians did not exactly welcome change, their religion did not remain static. Egypt was such a large nation that it had many independent regions with their own independent gods. If, through historical evolution, a region was merged with another, its gods might also be merged. Sometimes the characteristics of the local deity were identical or so similar to the principal deity that they were combined as one. If the local deity were particularly strong, it would not be absorbed completely but would become an aspect of the more important deity. Deities of different sexes might well become husband and wife, for example, or mother and son.

The Rise and Fall of Cults

Ancient Egypt represents three thousand years of history, during which time the importance of individual cults ebbed and flowed. Gods and goddesses tend to have overlapping functions, and they have composite names and conflicting attributes. When the local god Amun became fused with the creator god Re he became Amun-Re, the religious icon of one of the most powerful priesthoods the world has ever seen. As deities changed in importance, so the different creation myths that featured different deities in turn became more dominant.

RIGHT

*The priest Penmern'eb with the image of
the god Amun-Re in his form of a ram.*

One of the best-known creation myths is from the Egyptian city of Yunu, or On, which the Greeks called Heliopolis after their own sun god Helios. In this, the creator is one of the greatest of the Egyptian gods—Atum-Re, chief god of the Ennead, or nine deities of On, who is represented as a solar disc with hands at the end of its rays. According to the Atum creation myth, the other deitics are created when the Nile flooding starts to recede, exposing areas of high ground. Atum creates alone. He rises as a mound out of the primeval watery void and masturbates. (The Egyptians understood the role of semen in conception but not that of the ovaries or eggs.)

Nuit and Geb

Atum's hand acts as a womb for the seed and from this comes the first two divinities of the universe—Shu, god of light and air, and Tefnut, goddess of the realm of moisture. The union of Shu and Tefnut produces the divine couple of the sky goddess Nuit and the earth god Geb. The union of Nuit and Geb produces the principal deities of Isis, Osiris, Nepthys, and Set. From the divine union of these various gods and goddesses, other different deities are formed.

Isis

The goddess Isis presents an enduring and powerful image that transcends time. The classical world comes close to describing her complexity and beauty by giving her many names and titles. These include Isis Myrionymos (Isis of the Countless Names), the Pantocrateira (The Almighty), Isis Panthea (Isis of All Creation), Isis Sophia (Isis of Wisdom), Queen of Heaven, Great Virgin, Divine Mother, and Mistress of Magic. Many of Isis' images and titles were later adopted by the Catholic church to honor the Virgin Mary as Mother of God. Isis' special colors were black or blue: black was associated with the fertility of Egypt's black earth and blue was considered to be the color of female divinity.

Isis is strongly associated with water so she is also saluted as Isis Pelagia (Mistress of the Waves). In this manifestation she was invoked to keep boats safe at sea. When her husband Osiris was killed by their brother Set and his body scattered up and down the Nile, Isis sailed the river to recover the pieces. The tears of Isis as she wept over the remains of her slain husband were described as the annual Nile flood. At night, Isis sails on the boat of the sun god Re as he

journeys from west to east through the otherworld, protecting him with her potent magical spells so he can return to rise again the following day.

Isis the Magician

Isis is often hailed as the consummate wife and mother but, like many a mother, she is not above scheming on her son's behalf. One well-known Egyptian legend describes how Isis gains power over the sun god Re by discovering his secret name. In magical thinking, to know the true name of something or someone is to have power over it or them, which is why in many cultures people have secret names that are never used in public.

One day, when the gods and goddesses were walking in procession, Isis noticed a small bit of Re's spittle hit the ground. Seizing the opportunity, she gathered it up. Later, using her magic powers and the spittle, she created a poisonous serpent that she knew was the only thing that could harm the god of the sun. Knowing that Re strolled through his garden every day, Isis placed the serpent in his path and he was fatally bitten. Appearing as distressed as the other deities, Isis kneeled down and informed Re that she had the power to cast forth the poison from his body but only if he told her his true and secret name. Re was loath to reveal it. Twice he refused, offering instead a long string of titles, but Isis was unmoved and in the end he relented. Isis then received the name of power necessary to revive him. In this way, she was assured that her greatest ambition would be fulfilled—her son Horus would eventually rule all Egypt and wield the power of Re.

BELOW

A sailor in trouble could invoke the goddess Isis in the event of a bad storm.

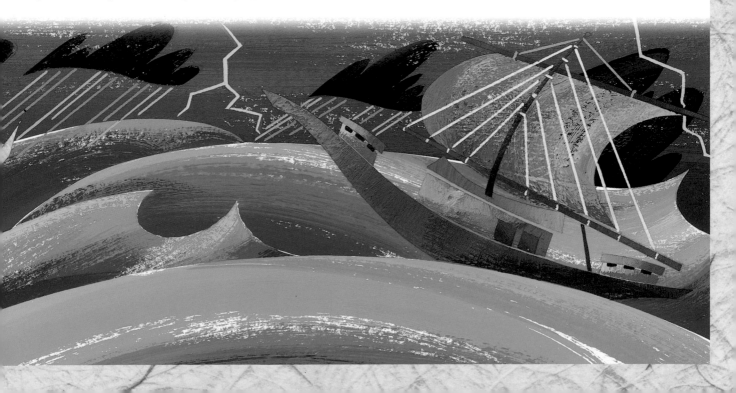

Isis—Deity for Womankind

Isis must have been a powerful role model for Egyptian women. She was independent, powerful, and wise, so her appeal to the middle-class business-woman in Memphis would have been strong. For the mother and wife in a small farming community in the western delta, she would have been the universal mother and the goddess to ask to protect an unborn child. For the young teenager in a Bedouin encampment in the extreme south of Egypt, the goddess could be called upon to charge up a small clay doll with power. Also, as Mistress of Magic, Isis would have known exactly how to incite the love of a young man.

Osiris

For the Egyptians, Isis and Osiris represented the perfect couple—devoted, loyal, dedicated, united, and very much in love. Although Narmer was the first historically recorded pharaoh, in myth Osiris was said to be the first King of Egypt. He ruled at a time when the gods and

LEFT
An image of Isis with a cobra upon her brow; cobras were seen as symbols of magic.

goddesses walked the earth. Osiris was a great giver of knowledge; he provided the people of Egypt with the knowledge of agriculture, animal husbandry, civilization and, above all, knowledge of the divine.

Osiris' benign and benevolent rule was cut short by the treachery of his brother, the god Sutekh. (Today we are more familiar with the Greek form of his name, Set.) At a lavish banquet held in honor of Osiris, Set presented a wonderful casket to the assembled company, which he said he would give to whoever fitted perfectly inside. As he knew the precise height of his brother Osiris, Set intended the casket to be his coffin. When Osiris stretched out in the casket, Set and his fellow conspirators slammed the lid shut, locking the bolts into place: Osiris suffocated and died. However, Set was determined that Osiris should be destroyed forever. He chopped his body into pieces and scattered them all over Egypt.

Isis searched for the pieces of Osiris' body and was assisted in her task by her sister Nepthys and Nepthys' son, the jackal-headed Anubis. Nepthys was well-suited to this role, for she is a goddess of the dead and holds the ankh, symbol of life, in her right hand. Nepthys was Set's wife, but she loved Osiris and the two sisters scoured Egypt, reassembling Osiris' body. Isis used her magic to revive Osiris just long enough for them to make love.

From the union of Isis and Osiris, the savior of Egypt was born. This was the god Horus, who defeated Set and avenged his father's murder. Horus

RIGHT
*A seated figure of Osiris. He wears the
double-plumed crown in his guise of Lord of the Dead,
New Kingdom, 22nd dynasty.*

embodies the ideal Egyptian son. He obeys and
reveres his father, fulfills the promise to continue a
funerary cult in his remembrance, protects and guards
his mother, and makes his father proud by continuing
his job extremely well—in this case, ruling over Egypt
as a powerful, benevolent, wise, and just pharaoh.

Osiris, King of the Kingdom of Death

Osiris continued to exercise kingship, but in a world
that mirrored this one—the land of the dead. He
became Foremost-of-the-Westerners, for the land of
the dead was believed to lie far beyond the western
horizon, where the sun entered the otherworld every
evening. As divine lawgiver, Osiris sat in judgment of
the dead in the great hall of truth of the otherworld.
Another title for him was He-Who-dwells-in-Orion.
Orion is Osiris' star. The Egyptians believed that the
night sky was the home of the chosen few who, when
they died, merited being transformed into stars.
Osiris is also god of vegetation and crops. His death
fits a common pattern in mythology, whereby a god
who introduces agriculture also symbolizes it in a
real way—he is cut down, replanted, and is reborn,
thus reflecting the cycle of the crops. Osiris' color is
green and this is seen to represent the ripening of the
crops; he is frequently shown with a green face in
Egyptian tomb art.

Sun Gods

There are three gods in Egypt who represent the sun, kingship, and creation—these are Atum, Re, and Amun. Atum, whose name means perfection, totality, and completeness, was important in the Old Kingdom when the nation's capital was in Lower Egypt near his cult center of Heliopolis.

Amun, whose name means "to conceal" or "that which is hidden," was originally a wind god venerated by Nile boatmen. He became the creator deity of the New Kingdom when the capital of Egypt was in Upper Egypt at Thebes. The Egyptians also referred to him as *asha renu*, He-who-is-rich-in-Names. Amun is represented as a human with a double feather crown, symbolizing his power over air and light. He is also represented as a ram or a goose.

Re

The sun god Re is the physical manifestation of the dynamic force of creation on earth. People only had to look up in the sky to see the sun god blazing overhead. They could experience at first hand Re's power in the energy, heat, vitality, and fertility that the sun represents. It is Re who creates human beings. Out of the receding waters of the Nile, Re emerges on a mound of earth called the *benben*. He cries out in the pain of creation and all humankind emerges from his tears as they fall to the earth. Although the god Re is the creator of all human beings, he is thought of in particular as the divine ancestor of the pharaohs, who gave the ruling family its religious legitimacy. In the same way that many royal families in Africa, pagan Europe, Polynesia, and Asia had their origins in the mythological union of a god and a human woman, so too did the pharaohs of Egypt. By the 5th dynasty, the most common title specific to the monarch was Sa Re, or son of Re. This was represented by the goose, the symbol for son. Re was then combined with Amun and worshiped as Amun-Re.

Khepri

As well as being the sun, Re has two other mythological manifestations that often appear in Egyptian

LEFT
Scarab beetles were associated with the sun god Re and rebirth. They appeared in tomb art and on jewelry.

art. One is that of Khepri, the scarab beetle, which has the curious habit of rolling dung into balls with its legs. This beetle is undeterred by obstacles, pushing its dung ball in a straight line with no deviation, just as the sun disk moves in a straight line across the sky each day. The word *kheper* means "becoming," or "being transformed" from one state to another, and may be equated with the idea of life and rebirth. The scarab beetle deposits its eggs in the dung and from this ball larvae can be seen emerging, just as Re the creator of humankind arose out of the *benben* or primeval earth.

ABOVE
A breast amulet showing the goddesses Isis and Nepthys venerating the scarab. New Kingdom, c. 1200 BCE.

Re-Harakhte

Re-Harakhte, the solar falcon, is an aspect of Re that is combined with the vigorous, youthful warrior god Horus, who is often seen as a falcon in flight. The name Harakhte is derived from the root word *akhet*, or horizon, a reference to the sun god appearing and disappearing over the eastern and western horizon with sunrise and sunset.

The word *horus* means "That-which-is-Above" and refers to the way in which the falcon patrols the skies. Horus' symbol is the falcon, a hunter after prey that strikes swiftly, silently, and without arousing the suspicion of its victims. Horus' archetype is solidly linked both with kingship and the sun and, as befits a golden monarch, his color is golden yellow. Horus is not strictly speaking a sun god, but over time he has become associated with sun gods and is often paired with them.

A Meditation on the Magical Goddess Isis

This is a simple meditation on the goddess Isis, queen of heaven and patron of the magical arts. Allow an hour for this exercise. You will need a quiet, softly lit room, where you can be alone. Remember to switch off your telephone so you are not disturbed while you are in the middle of your meditation.

Find a clean cloth to cover your altar. A white one is most appropriate, but another color that you find pleasing will work just as well. Cleanliness was extremely important to the Ancient Egyptians and cleanliness as a preparation for spiritual work even more so. There should be an image of the goddess Isis on your altar. If you have made the painting of Isis that we suggest at the end of Chapter 1 (*pp. 26–7*), then you can use this. If not, it is possible to buy statues of Isis from new age and museum

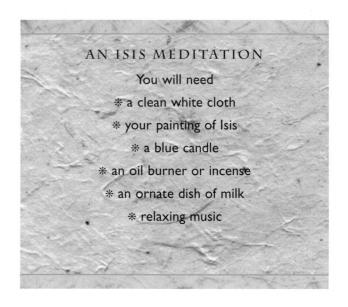

AN ISIS MEDITATION
You will need
✳ a clean white cloth
✳ your painting of Isis
✳ a blue candle
✳ an oil burner or incense
✳ an ornate dish of milk
✳ relaxing music

shops, and paintings of Isis on papyrus. Most city museums have Egyptian sections and mail-order services from which to obtain replicas of statues and other artifacts. (Museums are listed in Chapter 10.)

You will need a blue candle to symbolize the divinity of the queen of heaven and an oil burner or some incense. If these are difficult to obtain, then you could use a blue perfumed candle. You could use rose oil in your oil burner or burn church incense, a mixture of myrrh and benzoin, or Isis incense from a new age store. Beautiful smells have always been used in meditation and ritual to stimulate the psyche and to open us up to spiritual vision. You will also need a small ornate bowl or dish in which to place some milk as an offering to the goddess Isis. The milk symbolizes the life-giving and sustaining properties of the divine mother.

LEFT

Isis is a particularly relevant goddess to meditate on in these stressful times. She can calm and soothe the inner self.

Preparations

Create a simple altar by covering a small table, shelf, or windowsill with the white cloth. Place your image of Isis on the altar, together with the blue candle, perfume oil, or incense, and a small bowl of fresh milk. You might like to play soft music in the background as you meditate; the sounds of the seashore can be particularly relaxing. The goddess Isis is the goddess of mariners and her divine presence can be felt within the depths of the sea. To prepare for your meditation, start the music and light your candle. Take a sip of the milk and invoke her name three times. Isis is the Greek form of her name, but in Ancient Egyptian, she was Aset (pronounced "Ah-Set"). Intone, "Isis, Isis, Isis" or, if you would prefer the Egyptian, "Aset, Aset, Aset."

Relaxation

Before you begin, make sure the room is warm enough for you to sit still in comfort, but not too hot or you might become drowsy. Sit in front of your altar on a straight-backed chair, or you could sit or kneel on the floor. Try to keep your spine straight if you can. However, choose a posture that you can maintain without fidgeting. Relax and begin to focus on your breathing. Become aware of your inward and outward breaths as you inhale and exhale the breath of life, the divine gift to us from the gods. In your own time, allow your breathing to slow down, until you reach a gentle and relaxed rhythm. Now you are

ABOVE
Set up your altar to Isis with care. Lilies are particularly associated with this deity.

relaxed, you can prepare to begin the visualization exercise. The exercise is designed to take you into a meditative state. If you have been to relaxation classes or to yoga, this state of relaxed awareness where the psyche is open will be familiar to you. Once you achieve a meditative state, your mind will become relaxed enough to enter into a trancelike mode where the image and archetype of the all-mother, all-healing, all-protecting, all-powerful goddess Isis can become manifested through you.

Meditative Exercise

Close your eyes to begin with. You are going to visualize, one by one, the colors of the spectrum, from red, which symbolizes our raw animalistic energy, to violet, the color of spiritual tranquility and peace. Take time to visualize each color fully—do not rush.

Picture in your mind's eye the number 7 and the color red, the color of the rising sun. Allow red light to fill your psyche while you visualize the number 7. Stay with the red light for a few moments.

Next, visualize the number 6 and the color orange, the color of warm desert sand touched by the rays of the morning sun. Fill your mind with orange light, until it becomes bright and vivid.

Follow on with the number 5 and the color yellow, the color of the noonday sun. Remember to breathe slowly and evenly. With each number and color, feel yourself sinking down into a deeper state of blissful relaxation.

Continue with the number 4 and the color green, the green of the vegetation growing by the Nile.

Visualize the number 3 and Isis' own color of blue, the color of the summer sky.

Next, focus upon the number 2 and the color indigo, the color of a deep night sky that symbolizes the goddess, veiled and hidden.

Lastly, focus upon the number 1 and the color violet. Now we are beginning to pass out of the realm of earthly things. Allow violet light to fill your mind with gentle harmony and peace.

Affirmation

Breathe slowly and gently. You are in control and aware, while feeling relaxed and empowered. Affirm to yourself: "I am now in meditative awareness, where all I see is correct and balanced in accordance with the doctrine of the goddess Maat, goddess of the scales of harmony and justice, and of the goddess Isis—she upon whose breast I can rest my weary head and find peace and all-embracing love." Remain in

ABOVE
*Visualizing the colors of the spectrum will lull
you into a calm and meditative state.*

this meditative state and allow your mind to open itself to the free flow of images and feelings that reveal themselves to you. It may take several attempts before you begin to feel totally relaxed, but the resulting energy and the elimination of the harmful effects of stress will be your reward.

When you are ready to return to the everyday world, do not forget you are always in control. You can return in your own time whenever you wish. Simply count to yourself from 1 to 7, visualizing each color from violet back to red. When you are back with red, the color of physical energy, put yourself back in touch with your body. Flex the muscles around your neck and shoulders, stretch out your arms, and take a deep breath. Exhale and open your eyes to gaze upon the image of the goddess Isis upon the altar. Thank the goddess for her love and protection and then extinguish your candle and any incense. Drink some of the milk you have offered if you wish, keeping the rest to libate to the goddess. Repeat this exercise whenever you want to relax and feel at one with the goddess Isis and her powers.

A Libation to Isis

To libate is to return something to the earth. We do this to thank the goddess for what she has given us. You can libate the milk in your own back yard, a city park, or anywhere where you can touch the earth. If this is difficult, keep a pot of earth to use for libations. From time to time, take this earth outside and empty it out, refilling the pot again with fresh earth. This may seem a lot of effort simply to dispose of some excess milk, but it is important; when we have set something aside for a spiritual purpose we must treat it with respect.

LEFT
Before you begin this ritual, it is very important to enter a state of meditative awareness. Not only is this relaxing, it also makes your mind more receptive.

3

Magic and Amulets

The Egyptians referred to magic as heka. *Like Maat, heka is not only an abstract concept but also a god served by his own priesthood. Heka can change the course of fate. Even if it has been ordained that we will die of plague, that fate can be averted with the knowledge of Heka.*

Heka permeates all things. He resides in plants, animals, and human beings. Like any tool, his power can be used positively or negatively. Heka is important in maintaining the universe as we know it. Many ancient societies believed it was only the intervention of the gods that prevented the world disintegrating into chaos. Today we tend to take for granted that the sun rises and sets every day—the Egyptians did not. At dusk, the boat of the sun god had to descend into the watery, primeval chaos where the great serpent Apep or Apophis dwelled, along with a myriad other demons and evil spirits. Only the harpoon of Set, the presence at the rudder of Heka, and the strength and courage of Re, the sun god, could overcome the enemies of the light.

LEFT
*A statue of Thutmose I carrying two ankhs, the sign
of life, c. 1497–1425* BCE, *in Luxor Museum, Luxor.*

Sympathetic Magic

Sympathetic magic was a crucial part of Egyptian magical practice. In their magical world view, an image of a person, animal, or object that is blessed and consecrated with magical intent can take on the powers of the original—for good or ill. Although the crocodile is now extinct in Egypt, in the times of the pharaohs the Nile was infested with them. Crocodile attack was a common hazard so the usual way of cursing someone was to fashion a small model of a crocodile and cast it into the Nile with the intention that it would attack the victim when he or she was next at the riverbank.

On a more positive note, carved models of cows, calves, and trussed ducks and geese were placed in tombs to provide the deceased with plenty of meat and milk in the afterlife. The rich would also have model servants placed in their tombs so that they would continue to be served after death.

LEFT

An earthenware amulet of the Djed column—this was believed to represent the concepts of strength, endurance, and stability.

ABOVE

An Eye of Horus amulet would ensure certain resurrection after death.

Amulets

The idea that magical power and energy can be incorporated into an object to help us, protect us, or to attract certain energies toward us is an age-old one. Amulets, charms, and talismans are among the oldest archeological artifacts that we know. These objects are distinct from jewelry or other adornments in that they have a sacred, magical function that uses symbolic imagery to generate a magical purpose. Amulets are not powerful just because of their shape and design, but also because of the materials they are made from. The same principle applies today with birthstones. In modern astrology, the precious or semiprecious stone associated with each sun sign is considered to bring its wearer good fortune.

Magical Protection

The word amulet derives from the Latin *amuletum*. Amulets functioned as important tools for warding off trouble and aiding healing. The Egyptian word for amulet is *sah*, which has the same hieroglyph as the concept of protection. Amulets can be carried about the person, like a lucky rabbit's foot, or hung from the neck as a pendant, like the Christian cross. Nowadays, they can be purchased in many forms: rings, bracelets, brooches, and earrings can all be amulets in their own right. Important religious symbols elicit deep emotional responses from us, even if we are not consciously aware of it. In earlier civilizations, when they were not troubled by the scientific rationality of our own era, people were likely to have absolute faith in the efficacy of their amulets.

Amulet-making was a specialist trade. An amulet-maker was called a *Sah-oo*, which can be translated as "guardian or protector." Amulet-makers worked closely with doctors and healing priests and could be called in to help with patients, rather like a medical specialist is today. Amulets were not solely confined to healing, however. Heka was a neutral force, so amulet-makers could use their powers for good or for ill. Although each person had to account

for his or her actions in the otherworld after death, there seems to have been nothing to keep these magic specialists from performing harmful magic if the client paid the appropriate fee. Some magical texts specifically ask the gods for protection against amulet-makers' curses.

RIGHT
An attendant of the Temple of Rameses II at Abu Simbel holds up an ankh. Behind him is a gigantic head of Rameses.

Animals as Symbols

Amulets often used animal symbolism so that the wearer could access the animal's powers. The scarab beetle is an image that many people immediately associate with Ancient Egypt. Vast numbers of scarab amulets have been discovered during the past hundred years and enterprising merchants have a ready supply of convincing forgeries. Sacred to the sun god Re, the scarab would bring its wearer protection and the sun god's blessing.

The gazelle is fleet of foot and races over the savannah to escape its enemies. A gazelle amulet is one of the oldest amulets to be discovered in Egypt, and it may have been worn to bestow speed on the wearer. Hedgehog amulets are found in tombs and may have been used to bring life after death. In Egypt, the hedgehog lives in the desert at the edge of the cultivated fields. It hibernates under the ground in winter, and is seen to re-emerge in the spring. The rising from the ground was symbolic of the deceased being granted an afterlife. Some animal amulets might seem odd nowadays, although the symbolism was logical enough. The ordinary housefly was made into a gold amulet and presented to soldiers as a badge of merit; its persistence and determination in harassing beings so much larger than itself was considered an admirable trait in a member of the army.

Heket's Frog

Many amulets featured animals that were symbols of goddesses and gods. These include the cow, lion, hippopotamus, jackal, and frog. The frog represented Heket, goddess of fecundity and childbirth. In fact, one of the words for midwife in Egyptian was a "servant of Heket." Both the living and the dead

LEFT
A scarab breast amulet in the Egyptian Museum, Cairo. The hieroglyphs bear the name of the Pharaoh Psusennes I of the 21st dynasty.

LEFT
Golden flies were awarded as symbols of valor. From the tomb of Queen Aahotep at West Thebes, 18th dynasty.

could benefit from this amulet. Women who wanted protection in childbirth, especially during labor, would wear a frog amulet, for Heket could hasten the last stage of labor. It is worn today by devotees of Egyptian deities to bring divine assistance during a prolonged delivery. The Egyptians linked the frog with life, death, and rebirth; this explains its popularity as an amulet for the dead.

Body Parts as Amulets

Amulets representing parts of the human body appear in ancient cultures all over the world. They are still tied to icons in Orthodox churches in Greece to invoke a saint's healing powers. This is the same practice that would have been followed by an Ancient Egyptian woman or man. They would have taken an amulet representing the part of the body that needed healing to a healing shrine to create a

link between the sick individual and the source of healing. Body amulets were also used to assist the dead. Amulets of the eyes, ears, or tongue would give the gifts of sight, hearing, and speech.

Deity Amulets

Egyptians often wore amulets fashioned into the image of their favorite personal deity. Gold, silver, and electrum amulets were available for the wealthy, while glazed molded amulets were made to satisfy the poorer devotee. Nearly every deity known to the Egyptians could be fashioned into amulet form. The living or the dead could wear the amulets—both had need of their powers. Wearing an amulet in the image of the funerary god Anubis would be a help in acquiring the assistance of this god in the otherworld. His presence was vital in surviving the journey to the hall of judgment.

The Ankh

Symbols are often used as amulets. The ankh, the Egyptian looped cross that is also known as the *crux ansata*, was one of the holiest symbols of Ancient Egypt. In silver, gold, pewter, or plastic, it is still worn as an amulet today. In Egypt it remains the cross of the Egyptian Coptic Church, one of the earliest Christian Churches. As a hieroglyph, the ankh means "life"—either life in this existence or life eternal—so wearing an ankh is a powerful reaffirmation of the beauty and power of life itself. The ankh is associated with the two elements that the Egyptians believed were essential for sustaining life: air and water. The gods are frequently shown holding up the ankh symbol to the nose of a pharaoh or queen, bestowing life eternal through the medium of air. At other times, the ankh is shown with stylized streams of water, energy, or with small ankhs gushing forth to flow over the pharaoh.

No one knows for certain the origin of the ankh symbol. Early Egyptologists referred to the ankh as a "sandal strap." Another theory is that the top loop of the ankh represents a vagina and the crosspiece and central support symbolizes a

ABOVE

The god Atum, Lord of Heliopolis, opens the mouth of the dead pharaoh Senusert I to give him eternal life, Temple of Amun, Karnak.

penis and testicles. Together the loop and crosspiece create the ankh, forming a composite of female and male sexual organs that performs the greatest miracle of all creation—to bring forth life.

Eye of Horus

The word *udjat* translates as the "sound one" and represents the left eye of the falcon-headed god Horus. Horus' eye was ripped out of its socket when he did battle with his evil uncle, Set, to avenge the murder of his father, Osiris. The eye was cast into the sky and came to represent the moon. Thoth, the god of the moon and a healer, restored the injured eye and made it sound. The injured eye took 29 days to heal and the phases of the moon represented its healing. At the dark of the moon, it is most damaged. With the waxing moon it heals, until at full moon it is whole again. And so on. The powerful restorative powers of the Eye of Horus are revealed in the myth of Osiris. Horus offers his healed eye to his dead father and it is so powerful that it helps bring Osiris back to life. The Eye of Horus was buried with mummies to ensure certain resurrection in the afterlife. It was often painted on the prow of ships to protect them in their voyages.

Protection Against the Evil Eye

The Ancient Egyptians, like many traditional cultures, believed completely in the power that the evil eye could have over people. The "evil eye" is a glance or look designed to focus malevolent power upon a person and was thought to bring about a wide variety of misfortunes. An *udjat* amulet worn around the neck would ensure that its wearer was protected from all harm.

BELOW

An enamel glazed pottery Eye of Horus amulet from the late Dynastic Period, c. 600 BCE. This was thought to have strong restorative powers.

Making and Consecrating an Amulet

If you would like an Ancient Egyptian amulet, you can buy a ready-made image of a symbol such as an Egyptian goddess or god, an ankh, Eye of Horus, or scarab in the form of a necklace, bracelet, or ring, and consecrate it. Alternatively, you can go a step further and make your own amulet. Explore the properties of modeling clay (or a similar substance), which is available in toy, educational, and art stores; it molds easily into simple shapes

CONSECRATING AN AMULET

You will need

✳ an amulet of your choice

✳ a clean white cloth

✳ clean white clothes

✳ your Isis picture

✳ incense and a burner

✳ two blue candles

✳ two green candles

✳ a bowl of water

✳ a small ornamental bowl of salt

like ankhs and scarabs that can be hung from chains and worn around the neck. In either case, the important aspect of the magic is the consecration: without it, the amulet is simply a material object; after consecration it has psychological or magical power.

You may find that particular deities appeal strongly to you, and it may seem that they are calling you to them. In this case, it is a good idea to find or make an amulet in their image. Otherwise you might

LEFT

An earthenware amulet with the head of a lioness, either Sekhmet or Bastet. Note the Eye of Horus in the center, to further ensure protection with the flanking cobras.

LEFT
*Loose incense burned on charcoal produces a
more pleasant aroma than other forms of incense.
The burning charcoal must be rested on sand or
earth to protect the incense bowl from its heat.*

like to have an all-purpose protective amulet, such as an ankh, to protect you as you go about your daily life. If you do not want to make an amulet to wear, you could empower your Isis picture by consecrating it as described below.

Preparing a Room for Consecration

Before consecrating your chosen amulet, you will need to clean and tidy a room where you can perform your consecration, remembering that ritual cleanliness was of great importance to the Ancient Egyptians. You will need a small table or shelf that can act as an altar, which you can leave bare or cover with a clean cloth. Place your Isis picture on the altar. You will need incense and an incense burner; incense sticks can be used but loose incense that is burned on charcoal has a much more pleasant smell. (Esoteric stores often stock Egyptian incenses.) You will also need one or two blue candles for Isis and green ones for her husband Osiris, a bowl of water, and some

salt in a small ornamental container. You will need clean clothing—a long robe is ideal, but it can be any kind of garment. White or light-colored clothing is more typical of the dress worn in Ancient Egypt. You will also need some indoor sandals, or slippers that have not been worn outside. Alternatively, you can perform your ritual barefoot.

Preparing Yourself

Once you have prepared your sacred altar, you will need to prepare yourself. Allow an hour and a half for your ritual purification and ritual. Egyptian priests and priestesses prepared for every religious and magical rite with *wab,* or purification. The best way to prepare for a magical rite is to have a ritual bath. Perfume was important to the Ancient Egyptians and different scents have their own symbolism. In your bath you could include drops of perfumed oil, such as frankincense or lotus. The Ancient Egyptians used natron salt as a purifying agent and, following the same principle, salt can be added to a ritual bath to purify the water. Rock salt without additives is good for this purpose and can be obtained from health food stores. If you do not have a bath, shower instead.

An Affirmation while Bathing

Once you have prepared your bath, lie down in it and relax. Close your eyes and visualize the color blue. Against the blue background, visualize an image of the goddess Isis. (As an alternative, you could bring your Isis painting into the bathroom with you.) Visualize the wings of Isis stretching over you to protect you in your work. When you are ready, say the affirmation:

> *I prepare myself to enter a sacred space.*
> *May my spirit be cleansed of all negativity and may*
> *my heart be pure.*
> *As I draw upon the power of the element of water,*
> *may I draw upon the magic of the cosmos*
> *to protect and purify me in this my rite.*

As with every magical operation, the mundane is also important, so mirror this with a good physical wash. By washing the skin clean when we are about to do an important undertaking, we are preparing psychologically for what is to come.

When you have finished your bath, dry yourself and massage your body with oil or perfume. Stand before a mirror and say aloud:

> *Into me flows the power of Isis,*
> *the goddess who is the possessor of magic.*
> *She who performs magic and is effective of speech,*
> *may I be excellent of words.*

Your Consecration

To prepare your psyche for the rite, perform the meditative awareness exercise at the end of Chapter 2 (*pp. 40–1*). Close your eyes and visualize the colors of the spectrum one by one, beginning with red and the number 7. As your visualization reaches number 1 and the color violet, imagine that you pass out of the realm of earthly things. Violet light fills your mind with gentle harmony and peace.

Now imagine that your spine is an energized column of light. Your spine is the Djed column, or spine, of the god Osiris, the source of his strength and power. The column of light seems to reach higher and higher until it stretches to the heavens. From the base of your spine, the column of energy reaches down into the deepest heart of the earth, until you are joined to both heaven and earth. Now the power in your spine begins to build up and flow outward across your back and down into your arms. The light that is flowing from your spine is energizing your arms and hands. Take your amulet and allow energy from your hands to flow into the amulet, energizing it. You may see the amulet begin to glow with psychic energy. Now waft the amulet through the smoke of your incense saying:

> *I burn to you perfume, O Glorious Ones,*
> *I cense this shrine in homage to you.*
> *May this holy amulet be purified*
> *by the sweet-smelling incense of the gods.*

Now place the amulet on your open palms and offer it to your image of Isis, and the Isis and Osiris candles that surround it. Say aloud:

Hail to you, Isis and Osiris!
I ask your blessing and protection on this amulet,
by your holy power and love.
May this symbol guard and protect me
by night and by day.

May I walk under the sheltering wings of Isis
and with the strength of the Risen Osiris
be united with my innermost being.

Now put on the amulet and, in your own words, thank the spiritual forces that you have invoked. Extinguish your candles and return to everyday awareness by doing the meditative awareness exercise described at the end of Chapter 2 (*pp. 40–1*).

LEFT
During this exercise, imagine that your spine becomes illuminated with strong, energizing light.

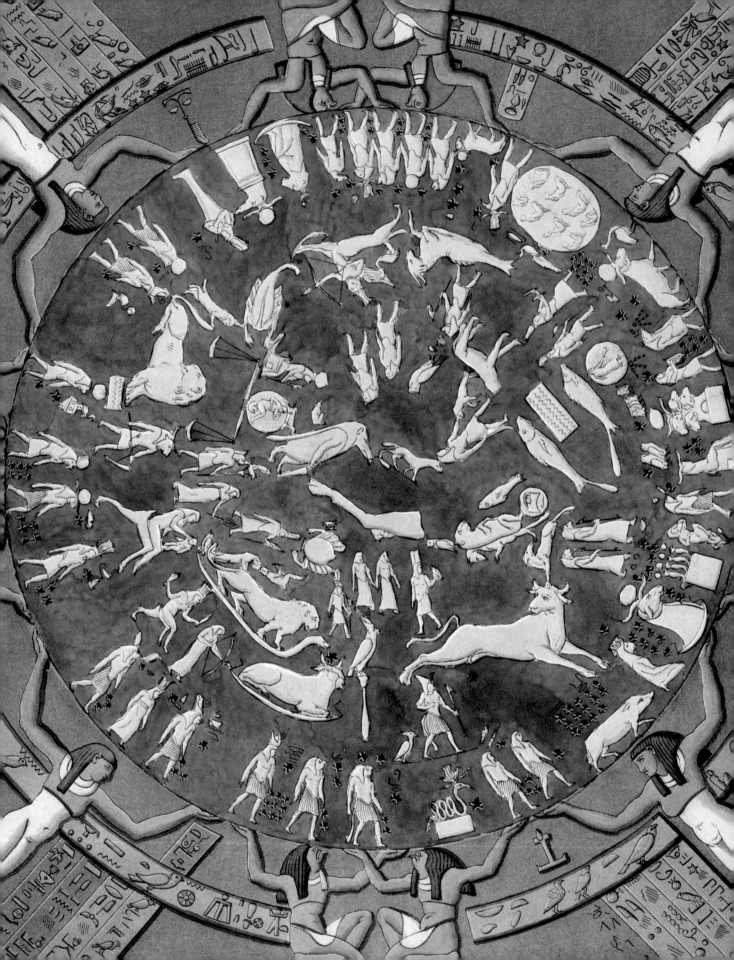

4

Astrology and Time

The Ancient Egyptians were keen astronomers who divided the year into a predictable pattern that was more accurate than anything devised by other contemporary peoples. In Egypt, two calendars ran simultaneously. One was based on the movement of the sun across the sky, the other on the lunar cycle.

The solar calendar consisted of 36 decans, or ten-day periods, that made up the year. This made 360 solar days, leaving five days unaccounted for. These extra days were placed at the beginning of the year and were celebrated as festival days that corresponded with the birthdays of Isis, Osiris, Nepthys, Set, and Horus. Each day and night was divided into twelve wenoot, or hours, each of which has a religious and astrological significance. The year was divided into three seasons of 120 days that related to the flooding of Egypt by the waters of the Nile. Akhet, or time of flooding, was around mid-July to mid-November; Proyet, or time of emergence, when the waters receded enough for plowing and planting to begin, was from mid-November to mid-March; and Shomu, dry time, when the grain would ripen and be harvested, was from mid-March to mid-July.

The Rising of Sirius, the Dog Star

The most important day of the Egyptian year was the helical rising of the star Sirius, or Sothis (known as Sopdet to the Egyptians), when the star is seen above the horizon as dawn approaches. The 70 days when Sirius is hidden from view below the horizon were important to the symbolism of Egyptian funeral rites.

Ba and Ka

The journey into the next world began at the moment of death. The spirit of the deceased was split into two entities; the Ba, or soul, which appears in Egyptian art as a bird with a human head, and the Ka, or etheric body. The deceased person's corpse meanwhile underwent the embalming ceremonies necessary to assist the Ba and Ka to live on. This process took 70 days and culminated in the ceremony of the "Opening of the Mouth." Using ritual tools, a priest opened the mouth of the deceased so that his or her senses could return in the form of the Ba and Ka. The Ka would remain in the tomb, the Ba could leave the tomb at night to visit former family or friends, and a third nonphysical component of the individual, the Akhet, would become the transfigured spirit that could ascend to the stars.

BELOW
Sunrise at the pyramids of Giza.

The Pyramids

The Ba, Ka, and Akhet could only exist if the physical body was preserved, so methods of doing this became a major preoccupation in Egyptian society. The Egyptian pharaohs' desire to live forever produced the pyramids—some of the great wonders of the ancient world. To obtain immortality it was necessary to harness the power of the stars. The means for doing so are found in the Pyramid Texts carved on the inner walls of the pyramids from the 5th and 6th dynasties (c. 2498–2345 BCE). Preserved in these texts are details of a stellar cult based on the constellation Orion, which the Egyptians called "Sah" and associated with the god Osiris. To become immortal, the pharaoh must become one with Osiris-Orion. This is described in the Pyramid Texts, numbers 820–2 (*see panel below*). Performed properly, the funeral rites enabled the spirit of the former pharaoh to become transformed into the Osiris King who would join as Orion with his wife Isis, represented by the star Sirius. A passage from the Pyramid Texts describes this: "Your sister Isis comes rejoicing in love for you. You have placed her on your phallus and your seed issues into her; she is ready as Sothis [Sirius]. And Horus-Sopdu has come forth from you as Horus-who-is-in-Sothis." The pharaoh becomes the risen Osiris, conqueror of death, and bears a son, Horus-Sopdu, son of Horus and Isis-Sirius.

BECOMING ONE WITH OSIRIS

Behold he has come as Orion,
behold Osiris has come as Orion.
O King, the sky conceives you with Orion,
the dawn light bears you with Orion.
You will regularly ascend with Orion
from the eastern region of the sky.
You will regularly descend with Orion
in the western region of the sky—your third is Sirius.

Archeoastronomy

The myths surrounding Sirius and Orion have been the source of much recent speculation by archeoastronomers. Archeoastronomers study temples and other monuments to establish whether ancient peoples deliberately aligned them to particular stars or solar phenomena such as the solstices in order to imbue them with spiritual and magical powers or to use them as astronomical calendars. For example, a convincing archeoastronomical theory explains the function of Stonehenge, in England, as an astronomical observatory. Archeoastronomy includes many prominent scholars but also many fringe theorists. For the non-specialist, it can be hard to distinguish between the two. One archeoastronomical theory put forward the idea that the pyramids are not just resting places for dead pharaohs, but that their placement on the ground is part of a grand plan that mirrors heaven upon earth.

The Great Pyramid

Followers of archeoastronomical theory have applied it to the case of the Great Pyramid of the pharaoh Khufu, who was known to the Greeks as Cheops. It was also a stellar temple that provided a stairway to the heavens above, so the king could ascend to his destiny as the resurrected Osiris. From the pyramid, the spirit of the dead pharaoh could journey through the heavens to Osiris' constellation, Orion, or Sah. Thus the pyramids are thought to have been built to align with the stars.

The Passage to Orion

Within the Great Pyramid are two chambers known as the King's Chamber and the Queen's Chamber. Investigation has revealed that there are curious shafts running at precise angles from the King's Chamber and Queen's Chamber toward the outside surface of the pyramid. A standard archeological explanation is that these shafts let air flow freely to construction workers in the chambers. An alternative and more mystical explanation is that the Ancient Egyptians wanted to provide a cool environment for the deceased pharaoh. Neither theory can be correct, however, because the shafts stop before they reach the outside of the pyramid and no holes to allow air in have ever been discovered. Neither do any other pyramids or tombs have air shafts: they were not an integral part of Old Kingdom funerary architecture.

As early as 1924, Egyptologist J. Capart proposed that the shafts had a symbolic function. Somehow they were an important part of the deification process through which the dead pharaoh was made a god— but nobody knew how. Alexander Badawy, a specialist in Egyptian architecture, was the first to suggest that the shafts may have been designed so that the spirit of the dead king could travel upward at an angle toward a fixed point in the heavens. Following the angle of the shaft from the chamber to the night sky,

LEFT

*The moon over the pyramid
of Khafre, Giza.*

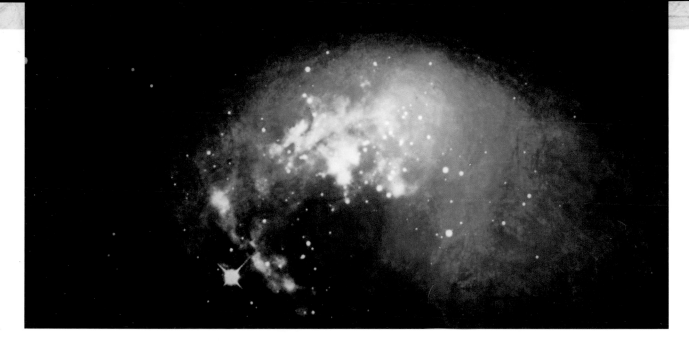

he found that the fixed point ended up on the constellation of Orion and, in particular, one of the stars in Orion's Belt. Perhaps these pyramid shafts were the means by which the spirit of the dead king was taken up to heaven to become one with Osiris-Sah.

In 1994, construction engineer and amateur Egyptologist Robert Bauval went one step further. He suggested that not only was the Great Pyramid pointing toward Orion but that it represented a particular star in Orion's belt. Furthermore, the other two pyramids at Giza, the Menkaure and Khafre Pyramids, represented the other two stars. This theory presumed that the Egyptians were capable of advanced surveying techniques so precise that they could site these enormous constructions in the exact shape of the constellation of Orion. Further speculation is that the entire landscape of Lower Egypt, where most of the pyramids exist, is an outline of the body of Osiris. Bauval goes even further, however,

and, comparing the Milky Way to the River Nile, argues that the relative distance of the belt of Orion from the Milky Way is mirrored in the distance of the pyramids from the River Nile.

Astrology

Astrology works on the principle that each of us is a unique component of the greater cosmos, born at a particular time, in a particular place, and with a destiny and purpose. The Egyptians were highly aware of the influence that the stars and planets above had on the individual—this features strongly in their myths. Like all divinatory systems, astrology has at its core the presumption that human life is predestined and predictable. However, if spiritual and magical knowledge can allow a person to predict the future, then it may be possible to change it. Unlike going into a trance, astrology is not a passive psychic discipline. It is a complex mathematical science that involves measurement, observation, and study of the stars and planets overhead.

Egyptian Astrology

The Ancient Egyptians had a keen interest in the stars, but they did not devise their own twelve-sign zodiac system. Instead, they adopted that of the Babylonians, the originators of the astrological system that is the basis for modern Western astrology. Claims that the Egyptians' astrological system predated that of Babylon began in 260 BCE when, in a battle of astrological one-upmanship, the Greeks said that the Chaldean system they were using was almost 500,000 years old. Not wishing to be outdone, the Egyptians put in a counterclaim—their system was at least 630,000 years old. Both claims, however, were nonsense: there is no evidence that the Egyptians ever devised their own system of natal astrology. However, although natal astrology based on the twelve signs of the zodiac did come fairly late to the Egyptians, they were keen observers of the night sky. We know that they recognized at least five planets: Mercury, which was known as Sebegu; Jupiter, which was known as the Bright Star; Saturn, which was known as Horus the Bull; Mars, which was known as Horus the Red; and Venus, which may have been known as the Morning Star.

LEFT
The Egyptians had identified five of the planets—Mercury, Venus, Mars, Jupiter, and Saturn.

The Denderah Zodiac

The most famous representation of the zodiac signs found in Egypt is the Denderah Zodiac. This was originally on the ceiling of the Osiris chapel at the Temple of Hathor at Denderah, but it was later moved to the Louvre Museum in Paris. The zodiac dates from the first century BCE and shows the twelve constellations that are familiar to us today, surrounded by other constellations and stars. There are some unusual features, however. Leo is depicted standing on a snake shaped rather like a boat, a reference to Re's night-time journey through the otherworld when he is threatened by the serpent Apophis; the human figures—Gemini, Virgo, and Aquarius—are all in Egyptian dress; the heavens are supported by twelve figures; four goddesses are positioned opposite the fixed signs of the zodiac—Taurus, Leo, Scorpio, and Aquarius; and four pairs of falcon-headed deities support the rest.

Predicting the Future

Human beings have always wanted to know when the cosmic tides are favorable for particular ventures, be they in love, battle, marriage, birth, business transactions, crop planting, or any of the other pre-occupations of human personal or political life. Modern astrology predicts whether or not days are favorable according to the interaction between an individual's astrological make-up and the position of the stars in the heavens on the day in question. Lacking a sophisticated system of natal astrology, the Ancient Egyptians were just as concerned to know whether a day would be favorable for a particular enterprise or not. The solution was a calendar that is known today as the Cairo Calendar.

ABOVE

A carving of a Horus falcon wearing the double crown of the pharaoh; Horus is associated with kingship and the sun. From the Temple of Seti I, New Kingdom, 19th dynasty, 1303–1290 BCE.

The Cairo Calendar

This was an essential document for anyone who wanted to avoid unlucky days while still taking full advantage of the lucky ones. The entry for each day is divided into three parts. The first part tells us simply whether the day is lucky, unlucky, partly lucky, or partly unlucky. The second part of the text explains why the day is favorable or not, for example, the birthdays of gods and goddesses were good days and those days that were the anniversaries of battle, conflict, or death were certain to be bad. On these unlucky days, people were encouraged not to do anything that would put them in harm's way. The third and last part of the entry gives advice on what or what not to do on that particular day. Even adverse days could have some plus points: people were often advised to take a day off work. Religious myths played an important part in determining the luckiness or otherwise of a day. Here are some examples from the calendar, taken from the translation made by Dr. Abd El-Mohsen Bakir in 1966.

Day 5 of the Third Month of Shomu

THE DAY: *Highly adverse.*

THE REASON: *It is the day of the departure of the goddess Hathor to the place from where she came. The gods are sad.*

ADVICE: *Do not go out of your home. Do not go on a boat. Do not do any work.*

Day 1 of the 1st Month of Akhet (New Year's Day)

THE DAY: *Very favorable.*

THE REASON: *It is the day of the birth of Re-Harakhte. The Nile begins to rise. All the gods and people celebrate.*

No special advice is given.

Day 3 of the 2nd Month of Proyet

THE DAY: *Very adverse.*

THE REASON: *It is the day of the going forth of Set and his confederates to the eastern horizon, and of the navigation of Maat to the place where the gods are.*

ADVICE: *Do not go out of your house on any road today.*

In the case of Day 3 of the 2nd Month of Proyet, the day is adverse because of the mention of the god Set. Set is god of chaos, destruction, illness, and all bad things. He is the antagonist of the good god Horus and on this day is marching with his confederates to the eastern horizon to do battle with the sun god Re or his protector Horus. As with any mention of a mythic battle, the day automatically becomes unfavorable. The reference to the goddess Maat, or Justice, going away "to the place where the gods are" would also be a warning to any Egyptian: do not go outside because you can expect no measure of justice or fair play. This was obviously a day to stay in bed!

When Unlucky Becomes Lucky

Despite the negative reputation of Set, in the context of the festival days his day is auspicious. Ancient mythologies did not look upon good and evil as absolutes in the way that we have been taught to in more recent religions. A particular energy could be good in one context and bad in another. Although Set can unleash chaos and destruction, these forces also destroy that which is outworn or corrupt. In its right place in the overall balance of things that is Maat, Set's energy is useful.

ABOVE
A symbolic unification of two conflicting powers, Horus (harmony) and Set (chaos).

A Ritual to Bring Good Fortune

This ritual is based on material for the final five days of the Egyptian year, which, taking the modern calendar into account, would be the beginning of the third week of July. However, the ritual can also be performed whenever you need a divine blessing. Perhaps you are sitting an examination or being interviewed for a job; perhaps it is your daughter's wedding and you want good weather and all to be harmonious. This rite is to help the day's currents of energy flow in the right direction. You can perform it three to seven days before the day in question.

Follow the exercise guidance at the end of Chapter 3 (*pp. 50–1*) to prepare your sacred space. Find a table to use as an altar and place it so that you can walk around it. To walk sunwise around an altar or sacred space creates a protective circle of energy around it. Cover it with a clean cloth. On your altar you will need five candles with candlesticks, or five nightlights. You will need blue for Isis, green for Osiris, dark blue for Nepthys, red for Set, and yellow or gold for Horus. Do not place your Isis picture on the altar for this rite because you want the energies of the five deities to be in balance. Place the candles in a downward-pointing equal-sided triangle, with the Isis candle to your right, the Osiris to the left, and the Horus candle below them to represent the divine mother, father, and child. Halfway along the line between the Isis and Horus candles, place the dark-blue candle of Nepthys. Halfway along the diagonal

ABOVE

In this ritual for good fortune, the five candles represent five deities associated with the five final days of the Egyptian year.

A RITUAL FOR GOOD FORTUNE

You will need
* a clean white cloth
* one blue candle
* one green candle
* one dark-blue candle
* one red candle
* one yellow or gold candle
* incense
* a bowl of clean water

between the Osiris and Horus candles, place the red candle of Set. The directions of right and left were significant to the Egyptians: left was the side of death, right the side of life. The breath of life entered the body through the right ear and at death exited through the left ear. You also need incense to represent the element of air, and a bowl of clean water to represent the water element. You may prefer to use bottled spring water for ritual purposes.

Preparation

Allow an hour and a half for the rite and take your ritual bath or shower before you begin. Clean your sacred space, wash yourself, then sit or stand before your altar and perform the meditative awareness exercise at the end of Chapter 2 (*pp. 40–1*).

BELOW
The Ancient Egyptians considered ritual purification and cleanliness to be an essential preparation for magical deeds.

Beginning your Rite

To begin your rite, consecrate and cense your sacred space by circuiting the altar clockwise. Take your water bowl and, starting from the back of your altar, walk clockwise in a complete circuit around it, sprinkling water on the ground as you go. You can use these words of blessing:

O great gods and gentle goddesses of the land of Khemet. I make this offering of water to prepare a temple for your worship. May this circle be a barrier that no evil presence or thought can break. I do this in the name of Maat. May my voice and intention be true and my heart pure.

Return the water bowl to the altar and take your incense burner and process around the altar as before, holding it up to allow the incense smoke to consecrate your sacred space, saying:

O great gods and gentle goddesses of the land of Khemet. I make this offering of incense to prepare a temple for your worship. May this circle be a barrier that no evil presence or thought can break. I do this in the name of Maat. May my voice and intention be true and my heart pure.

Return the incense burner to the altar. Stand facing the altar, open your arms out at shoulder height, your palms facing the altar, and ask out loud for the blessing of the gods:

I perform this rite in the names of the Ennead of On:
Atum-Re, Shu, Tefnut, Nuit, Geb,
Isis, Osiris, Nepthys, and Set.
May they and their heirs:
Horus, Bast, Anubis, and the Sons of Horus,
be favorable unto me.
May my Divine Father Geb be my foundation;
may he be strong beneath my feet.
May my Divine Mother Nuit be my protection;
may the arch of her body shelter the universe.

These words will focus your mind on what you are asking of the gods, and make your request more sincere. Now address your thoughts to the gods and ask that they will bless you and your endeavors on the day in question. You might say something like:

Gracious Goddesses and Gentle Gods who rule the universe,
I ask your blessing on [date] when I must perform the difficult task of [state your purpose]. Help me to perform this task, drawing on your energy and strength. May the time be favorable to me and mine and may fortune assist me.

Now meditate for a few moments on the day to come. Visualize yourself completing the day successfully with no obstacles or problems standing in your way. Finally, address the gods once more to thank them for their blessing.

Hail to you, O Great Ones,
according to your names—
children of a goddess,
who have come forth from the sacred womb,
lords by virtue of your father,
goddesses by virtue of your mother,
who do not know the necropolis, the place of death.
Behold, may you protect and save me,
may you make me prosperous and safe;
for I am a servant of the gods
and my love is with you forever.

To end your rite say:

I thank the great gods and gentle goddesses of the land of Khemet,
for their presence in this temple of life.
As your force and power return to the cosmos,
may your eyes, ears, and hearts be favorable unto me.

Extinguish your candles and return to the everyday world. Place your candles somewhere where you can light them for a period each evening until you have reached the day for which you seek blessing.

LEFT
Burn your candles a little more each day until you reach the day when you need good fortune.

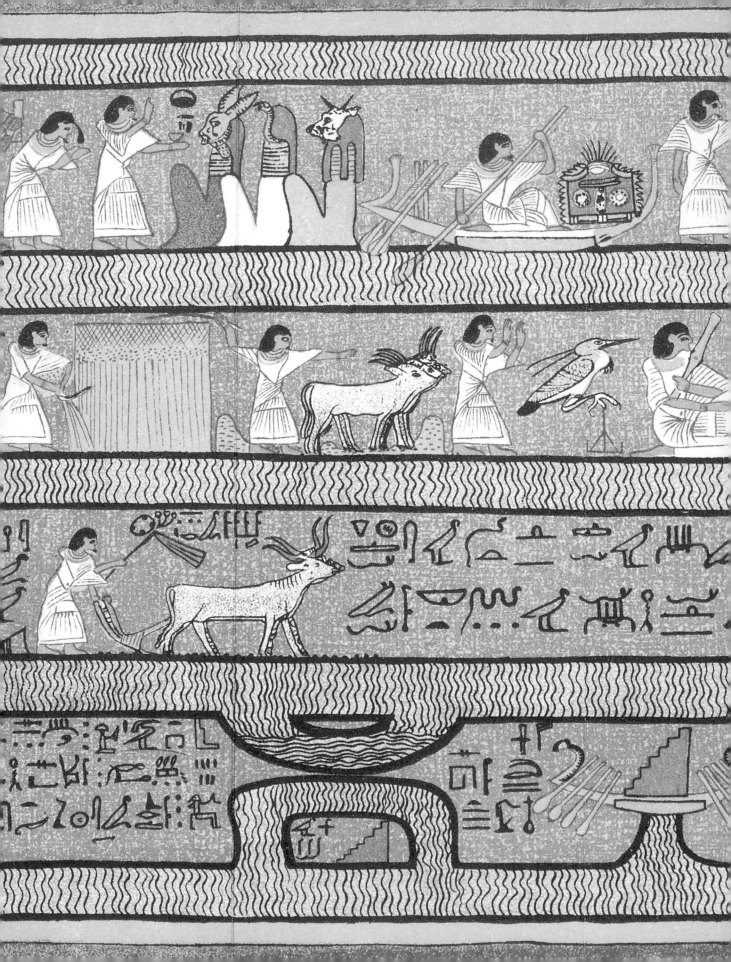

5

Language and Hieroglyphs

Ancient Egypt was a land rich in natural resources—minerals and metals, cattle and corn. Even more important for Egyptian civilization was one of the greatest gifts of the Nile, the long, slender marsh plant with fan-like flowers that the Egyptians called mehyt, *and we call papyrus. Papyrus was the source of the world's first paper.*

Until the advent of the computer age, all governments relied heavily on paper records. Papyrus enabled the Egyptians to create files, lists, inventories, deeds, legal contracts, and accountancy records—all the office systems of a sophisticated, efficient state. The Egyptians had plenty of papyrus for their own use, and it become a useful export to neighboring states. Egyptian writing was in the form of pictures, which we call hieroglyphs, from the Greek for "sacred writing." For the Egyptians, writing was a magical activity imbued with mystical power. The sacred quality of hieroglyphs was enhanced because they were used to commemorate special occasions, by carving them onto a hard material, like stone or wood, with the specific intention that they survive for all eternity.

LEFT
An illustration from the Book of the Dead *showing a life that combines the magical with the mundane—from bowing before the gods to tilling the fields.*

THE EGYPTIAN ALPHABET AND CORRESPONDING SOUNDS

SIGN	SOUND	OBJECT DEPICTED	SIGN	SOUND	OBJECT DEPICTED
	guttural A	Egyptian vulture		CH (as in "loch")	placenta (?)
	Y	flowering reed		ICK (as in "tick")	animal's belly with teats
	I (as in "igloo")	two reed flowers oblique strokes		S	bolt
	AH	forearm		S	folded cloth
	WAH or OO	quail chick		SH (as in "ship")	pool
	B	foot		K	hill-slope
	P	stool		hard K	basket with handle
	F (as in "father")	horned viper		hard G	stand for jar.
	M	owl		T	loaf
	N	water		TCH (as in "witch")	tethering rope
	R	mouth		D	hand
	H (as in "hair")	reed shelter in fields		J (as in "jump")	snake
	H (as in "harvest")	wick of twisted flax			

ANCIENT EGYPTIAN MAGICAL VOCABULARY

SIGN	EGYPTIAN WORD	MEANING	SIGN	EGYPTIAN WORD	MEANING
	Seh-Wer	curse		Ka	spirit/life force
	Sheni	exorcise		Sopdet	the star Sirius
	Het-Netcher	temple		Sutekh	animal of Set
	Heka	God of Magic		Sutekh	animal of Set recumbent
	Ah-Set Neferet Netcheret	Isis Beautiful Goddess		Sutekh	the god Set
	Wasir Nefer Netcher	Osiris Beautiful God		Henenoo	turmoil (note the animal of Set determinative)
	Ahset	Isis (note the egg to further denote female)		Neshni	storm or to rage (note the animal of Set determinative)
	Senetcher	incense		Heka	Magic
	Hery-Hebet	lector priest		Djheuty	the god Thoth
	Hem-Netcher	prophet/chief priest		Hesek	disease demon
	Wab	purification priest		Sau	amulet-magician
	Hem-Ka	soul priest		Sah	amulet
	Soonoo	doctor/physician		Peh-Netcher	sorcery

Lost and Found

As Ancient Egypt was invaded first by the Greeks, then the Romans, then the Arabs, people forgot the meaning of the beautiful pictorial writing. Although hieroglyphs endured on temple walls, coffins, and in myriad other ways for around 1,400 years, their meaning was lost. The last known hieroglyphic inscription was made in 394 CE. It was not until the 18th century, when Napoleon conquered Egypt, that a chance find revealed the secrets of the hieroglyphs. An important part of Napoleon's military entourage was a team of scholars entrusted with discovering and recording every Ancient Egyptian artifact they could find. One of the most important finds was the Rosetta Stone. From this, the baffling code of the Egyptian language was deciphered.

ABOVE

The Rosetta Stone was inscribed with hieroglyphs in Demotic Egyptian, with Greek translation. Comparing the two gave scholars the key to understanding the Ancient Egyptian language.

The Egyptian Alphabet

Our ancestors were logical in the way that they named the world around them. Often the Egyptian name of an animal was similar to the noise it makes. For example, the word for ass is (🐂) pronounced "Ah-Ah." The next stage in linguistic evolution happens when pictures of things are used as individual sounds and groupings of sounds form words. From this, an alphabet develops. For instance, the great predynastic king responsible for uniting Egypt for the first time is called King Narmer. Archeologists know his name because a large slate carving was discovered with the figure of a king destroying his enemies with the help of the Horus falcon, an important totem of kingship. Above the king's head are the two glyphs Nar (⬌), which appears to be some kind of fish, and Mer (𓌹), a chisel.

Egyptian hieroglyphs indicate objects as well as abstract concepts. The glyph (☉) can be used to mean the sun, as well as the name of the god Re. Feathers are associated with the goddess Maat and the glyph of the ostrich feather (𓆭) can symbolize the idea of divine justice and harmony, as expressed through the concept of Maat.

Simple Translation

Ideograms are placed with certain verbs. A noun is a person, place, or thing, a verb is an action, and hieroglyphs were adjusted to reflect this. For example, the noun "boat" has an ideogram showing that the word in question is indeed a boat. The word is made up of three consonants "d," "p," and "t" (🖼). The verb "to sail" (🖼) is composed of two consonants, "h" and "d," and has the picture of a boat as a determinative because it shows, or determines, the meaning of the verb. Even without knowledge of Ancient Egyptian, you can begin to guess the meaning of a sentence by looking out for the ideograms and determinatives.

ABOVE

A model of a funerary boat, stuccoed and painted wood, Middle Kingdom, c. 2000–1900 BCE.

Words of Power and Magic

Egyptian spells begin instructions on how to intone sacred words with the phrase *djed medoo*, or the "words to be spoken." The importance given to the power of the spoken word in magic is indicated by the name for magic itself, Heka. Often the determinative used to illustrate Heka is a glyph of a kneeling man with his hand to his mouth (🖼). This specifically relates to the power of speech. The power of the spoken word is also closely associated with the goddess Isis, whose own cunning ruse discovered the secret name of Re and obtained power over him:

> *I am Isis the goddess,*
> *the possessor of magic,*
> *who performs magic,*
> *effective of speech,*
> *excellent of words.*

LEFT

Ostrich feathers were greatly prized and were a symbol of the goddess Maat.

Petitioning the Dead

In Ancient Egypt, where only the minority of people could write, words were considered powerful tools. The spoken word could be used in many spells for magical intentions; the written word was thought to reach into the realms beyond and could be used to talk with the dead. An ancient idea common to most early societies, and still found in many cultures today, is that our ancestors can assist us with problems in everyday life. Many cultures have shrines to their ancient ancestors. In part they are commemorative, like war memorials or gravestones, but in the past they were also places where people could petition the dead for assistance and guidance. As the dead had been released from the confines of the physical body, it was thought that they had a knowledge that transcended the boundaries of time and space.

Letters to the Dead

The Egyptians believed that dead family members would take the same interest in them once they were in the afterlife as they had in the everyday world. They were therefore frequently asked for help through "letters," messages written on clay bowls that were then fired. The bowls would be filled with food and left as offerings to the dead person whose intercession was sought. Often the messages are sketchy and simple because people assumed that their dead relatives still knew what was happening in the world of the living. One example is on display in the Louvre

Museum in Paris. It is a request from a woman named Merti to her dead son, who is called Mereri. After long flowing phrases of flattery, she gets to the point. It seems Merti and her children are embroiled in a legal dispute and must go to court; we do not know for what reason, but it could be a will or land dispute. Merti is worried about the outcome and, as a safeguard, she appeals to her dead son to speak on her behalf in the otherworld before the tribunal of the gods. She believes the decision will be in her favor.

Another message is an appeal for healing. An elderly servant named Imiu has fallen ill. She lives in the house of a man who has recently died; he was a priest named Antef, who was the son of a man called Iwanakht. The petitioner, Dedi, writes a letter to the dead man on behalf of the ill servant. "As for this serving-maid Imiu, who is sick, you do not fight for her night and day with every man and woman who does harm to her. Do you want your household to be desolated? Fight for her today anew so that her household may be established and so that water may be poured for you. If you do not help, then your house will be destroyed." As a loyal servant, Imiu might have been expected to make offerings, or to

ABOVE
It was important to remember the dead. Offerings of fruit and other foods were made by relatives to give them sustenance in the afterlife.

"pour water," to the dead Antef. This was an important obligation for a deceased person's heirs to fulfill; they would present offerings of food and drink, such as bread, fruit, and beer. This is a good example of the Egyptian belief that illness can be caused by ill-wishing. Perhaps the servant has received something in the will of the deceased and other family members are resentful. The ability of the dead to intercede on behalf of the living in the otherworld is the motivation behind the numerous letters to the dead that have been discovered by archeologists.

Sacred Chants

Chanting the names of our deities is one of the oldest ways of honoring them. It also has a powerful effect on the human psyche. Even if we are unfamiliar with a particular religious tradition, chanting can move our emotions in all sorts of ways. An African war chant can rouse us to anger, a Tibetan Buddhist chant can generate a feeling of profound peace, a Native American chant can move us to tears, and a chant by the medieval mystic Abbess Hildegard von Bingen can lift the spirit into the highest realms, even if the meaning is unknown to us and the spiritual tradition is different from our own. The emotions and spiritual longings of humankind are expressed in that most human of instruments—the voice.

Chanting Sacred Words

A powerful way of linking to Ancient Egyptian deities is to chant their names. You have already done this in the Isis visualization exercise in Chapter 2 (*pp. 40–1*) when you chanted her name as Isis or Aset. Pronouncing Ancient Egyptian words might seem daunting, but they were written phonetically and the same principle is applied when writing Egyptian words in our own alphabet. Providing you break the words down into syllables, they are easy to pronounce. The name of the sun god Amun-Re is pronounced "Ah-Moon-Rah." If you are used to singing or chanting, you can adapt your own techniques to chanting deity names. If not, here is a method that you can use.

To chant the name Amun-Re, take a very deep breath and sing a note at whatever pitch, high or low,

LEFT
Six baboons and the goddesses Isis and Nepthys venerate the lifegiving power of the sun god. The goddesses are seated upon the symbol for gold and face the Djed column of stability.

that feels comfortable for your voice. Chant slowly and evenly, "Ah-Moon-Rah," giving equal emphasis to all three syllables. Breathe out as you sing the note, letting it continue for as long as feels comfortable. Then take a long, slow, deep breath inward, filling up the diaphragm completely before beginning the chant all over again. You can repeat this a number of times before stopping. Chanting in this way can be a powerful experience. The outside world is blotted out by the vibrating sound within our bodies of a name of the divine.

LEFT

A sarcophagus figurine fusing the three gods Ptah (creation), Sokar (fertility), and Osiris (death). Small copies of the Book of the Dead *were kept in these.*

Once you have practiced chanting divine names, you might like to try some phrases. It is best to keep the words to a few syllables; too many and they can become easily jumbled and confused. To call upon the goddess Isis to manifest her power, chant the phrase, "Aset neferet netcheret" (　), which means "Isis, beautiful goddess." The way to pronounce this would be "Ah-Set Ncf-fer-ret Net-Chur-Et." Instead of chanting the phrase using a single note, you could try creating a few notes to sing it.

Experiment with different tunes. Sometimes you might want to sound solemn, at other times joyful. You can modify your chant depending on your mood, on which god or goddess you are invoking, and to reflect your hoped-for outcome. It is a very personal choice. You can also call upon the god Osiris. The Egyptian form of the name Osiris is Was-Sur. To chant the phrase "Osiris, beautiful god" (　) say: "Was-Sur Nef-fer Net-Chur."

The difference between this phrase and the chant to Isis is that Egyptians use the "t" sound as a feminine word ending. To indicate feminine nouns, the hieroglyphs also add the glyph for loaf of bread (　). For example, examine the following words: *Sa* (　) means "brother," *Sat* (　) means "sister," *Bak* (　) means "manservant," *Baket* (　) means "female servant." In divine names, to emphasize the divinity of the feminine force of creation, the hieroglyph of an egg is added beside the "t" glyph (　).

Dawn Ceremony

This exercise should ideally be performed somewhere where you can see the sunrise, but if this is not possible you can visualize it instead. Before going to bed, check in a newspaper to find out the time of sunrise. Depending on how quickly you like to get out of bed and get ready, you will need to set your alarm about an hour and 20 minutes before dawn. Allow 20 to 30 minutes for the ceremony itself.

When you get up, have your ritual bath or shower. You must be dressed and ready to begin the exercise before dawn. Go and sit in your chosen spot to watch or visualize the sunrise. You may like to burn incense or play soft music. Once you have made yourself comfortable, relax and breathe calmly. If you do yoga, you could begin with some yoga exercises and include the Salute to the Sun. Lastly, perform the meditative awareness exercise, so that you are fully prepared mentally.

Saluting the Sun

Wait and watch as the sun begins to light the distant horizon. As you see the sun disc rise (or visualize this at the appropriate moment if you cannot see it), imagine the sun god appearing in the form of a great falcon silhouetted against the glowing disc of the rising sun. Here the sun god Re is fused with his grandson Horus in the form of Re-Harakhte, the solar falcon, Harakhte being derived from the word *akhet*, or horizon. As the sun appears, intone the following chant out loud: "Ah-Ha Rah Ha-Rekh-Tay." This means "All-hail! Re who rises above the horizon." This fusion of the god Re with Horus is shown by an image of the sun god with the head of a falcon surmounted by a solar disc.

Prayers to Deities

You might like to say a prayer to the sun god to help you in your daily life. If you want to address an Egyptian deity, you can find invocations in translations of Egyptian texts such as the *Book of the Dead*. You can also create your own. Many people today venerate the deities of Ancient Egypt, writing poetry, prayers, and hymns of praise to them, or simply talking to them in heartfelt words. If you would like to use some words that have been used by others, here is a modern prayer of praise to Re.

Sit for a while with the rays of the morning sun bathing your body, being careful not to look directly into the sun. Then, to finish, chant the name of Re the rising sun a few more times: "Ah-Ha Rah Ha-Rekh-Tay." This is a good exercise to perform when you are about to start a new enterprise and need positive, creative solar energy in your life.

RIGHT
The pyramids of Giza lift our consciousness toward the heavens, where the rising sun has illuminated them for thousands of years.

A PRAYER TO RE

Hail, O Re, in your rising!
You come forth to give us day,
O my Lord of the Sun.
You rise above the horizon of the land,
and your light bathes Earth and Heaven.
Your rays of amber and gold
enter the temples and hearts of your people,
and they are glad.
O Great God Re,
who comes forth in the form of the sun,
and rises up in majesty to give us light and life,
I praise you, O Re.
May your rays enter into my heart.
Grant that I may build a temple
to you in my spirit,
and that it may be your dwelling place, O Re.
Furnish my temple with joy, O Re;
let your light enter me,
filling me with your love and warmth,
your energy and your power.

6

Sex and Love Magic

The closest equivalent to our word "literature" in Ancient Egyptian is medet neferet, *or "beautiful words." The French words* belles lettres *come close to the Egyptian notion that the use of language is one of the highest forms of art. The literary outpourings of the Egyptians include folktales, wisdom literature, myths, legends, and something with enormous popular appeal—love songs.*

The lyre or the harp probably accompanied the song lyrics, with percussion provided by cymbal, tambourine, sistrum, or drum. Fifty-four love songs have been discovered so far. These allow us more than ever before to understand and identify with the Ancient Egyptians. They had none of our society's recent inhibitions about the expression of sexuality; a loving eroticism was a normal part of life, and the abundance of love songs and spells shows that gaining and keeping the attentions of one's beloved was an important preoccupation for both women and men.

LEFT
The young Tutankhamun walking in the royal garden to meet one of the daughters of Akhenaten. She holds the mandrake flower, which has great erotic significance in Egyptian art and implies that they may be lovers.

Young Love

Before marriage, young Egyptians had considerable sexual freedom. The love songs reveal the typical rendezvous that young lovers could escape to— under a pomegranate tree, in a tent, or even the local cemetery, a popular courting place in rural Europe until recent years. In the Egyptian language, one euphemism for lovemaking was "building tents." There is none of the complicated game playing or elaborate phrases of courtship that one finds in the love songs of other cultures. Egyptian life was much more earthy. When a young couple found themselves alone, their mutual passion for each other resulted in spontaneous sex that was considered neither vulgar nor a cause for shame.

It was common for the pursuit of the beloved to be compared to birds flying, animals running, and to ways of entrapment. A young man mentioned in a song in the Harris Papyrus is described as a stallion on the track, or a falcon swooping into the papyrus marsh. Women are frequently compared to a variety of fruits or other plants that are known for their sweetness and juiciness, or that possess specific flowering beauty, like the mandrake.

Women's Love

Women wrote equally passionate love songs to men. One good example is recorded in the Harris Papyrus. Lovers often referred to their partners as a brother or sister. This does not mean they were committing incest but that they were acknowledging their partner as the brother or sister of their soul. (The use of the brother and sister terminology between lovers is also found in the "Song of Songs" in the Bible.) The young woman has been creating a garden and speaks of this to her love.

RIGHT

The mandrake was a common symbol in Egyptian love poetry. Fair maidens were compared to the beautiful, delicate blooms of the plant.

AN EGYPTIAN LOVE SONG

There are saamu flowers in it,
before which we are glorified.
I am your foremost sister,
I am yours; as is the acre of land,
that I made to flourish with flowers
and all manner of sweet-scented herbs.
Pleasant is the channel in it,
which you dug with your own hands
for our refreshment in the north wind,
a beautiful place for walking hand in hand.
When we are together,
my body is satisfied and my heart rejoicing.
Hearing your voice is pomegranate wine—
when I hear it I am alive. Whenever I see you,
it is better than food and drink.

Love Spells, Charms, and Talismans

Young Egyptians were as focused on obtaining a partner as young people are today, so folk magicians could make a good living from providing them with spells to attract the object of their affection. Where persuasion and love songs were ineffective, passionate lovers might resort to less scrupulous means of getting their desired partner. In Egypt, a classic figurine used for love magic was made in the form of a bound and kneeling captive: these were usually women and would have been made by men. A variety of materials was used, including alabaster and wood, but usually they were made from wax or clay. In several of the surviving clay figurines, there are holes by the bound hands to indicate that a cord or thread would have been tied around them. As the threads bound the object of the maker's passion, so would she be bound in love to him.

Hathor, Goddess of Love

The goddess Hathor, or Het-Heru, is the supreme goddess of love, sensuality, dance, and pleasure. Hathor is carved or painted in several ways. As a woman, she stands tall and sinuous, and on her head is her hieroglyphic emblem or cow horns, sometimes with a sun disc. In this form she is indistinguishable from the goddess Isis, who is shown in a similar fashion. A cow can also be used to symbolize Hathor.

A piece of New Kingdom sculpture showing Hathor as a divine cow is one of the most beautiful examples of Egyptian art and shows the cow goddess emerging from a field of papyrus. Her udders are full of milk and are symbolic of the mother's milk that provides a child with sustenance. The pharaoh Amenhotep II is depicted in the sculpture being suckled by this protective goddess. Another image, which adorns the capitals of columns at the mortuary temple of Deir El Bahri and appears on sistrums, is of Hathor with a human face and cow's ears.

A Divine Couple

Hathor and Horus are closely linked in Egyptian myth. The Egyptian form of her name, Het-Heru, translates literally as "mansion of Horus." The "mansion" may refer to Hathor's womb, for in the earliest myths it was she, not Isis, who was the mother of the god Horus, and Horus' father was Re, not Osiris. This would be symbolically consistent since both Re and Horus are solar deities and are depicted with the heads of hawks. Indeed, images of the cow goddess long predate any archeological evidence for Isis or Osiris. A cow-headed goddess is even shown flanking the first pharaoh of Egypt on the Narmer slate palette, so it can be seen that the Egyptian pharaohs and Hathor were closely linked in the earliest period of Egyptian history. Others myths refer to Hathor as the wife of Horus. Together, Hathor and

BELOW
Three bronze Apis bulls and a Hathor cow, Late Period, 7th–6th-century BCE. *Most Egyptian deities were associated with an animal symbol. The cow was the symbol of Hathor, goddess of Love.*

LEFT
*All aspects of life had deities—from solemn
to joyful. The goddess Hathor, with her emblem of
goddess of the west, and Horus of the horizon,
the falcon god, are paired in this tomb painting.*

there overnight to receive holy visions. During excavations of the worker's village of Deir El Medineh, not only was this stela discovered but also more than 19 scrolls of papyrus that made up the private library of Qen-her-khepeshef. Purchased in the early 20th century by the millionaire Chester Beatty, they are known as the Chester Beatty Papyri and include a text on medicine that is in the British Museum.

Worship of the benign goddess Hathor continued into the Greek period. At this time a massive new temple was built to replace the earlier structure of the Temple of Hathor at Denderah, one of Egypt's most interesting sights and the original home of the Denderah zodiac. The plan of the Ptolemaic temple illustrates the associations Hathor had with water and healing. As well as the sacred lake usually found next to temples, there is a room divided up into small chambers. Pilgrims wishing to remain in a state of darkness and meditation to receive healing or visions from Hathor may have secluded themselves in these. A corridor leads from the chambers to a series of basins used for ritual bathing and healing baths. This water from the sacred lake would have flowed over statuettes of the goddess inscribed with magical healing spells, but these no longer remain.

Horus produce a child, Ihy, who is lord of music and ecstasy; he is also lord of beer. Ihy's cult symbol is the sistrum; another god that is linked to music.

Hathor of Healing Visions

Hathor was connected primarily with love, but she was also appealed to for her healing powers. One of the most interesting archeological finds that connect Hathor with healing belonged to a scribe called Qen-her-khepeshef in the 19th dynasty. He is shown on a finely carved stela with his knees bent and his arms held up in adoration of the goddess Hathor. Upon this sculpture it is written that Qen-her-khepeshef traveled to the sanatorium of Hathor to drink the water for health and inspiration and remained

Glamor Rites

Magic has often been used to improve attractiveness and self-confidence. The Glamor of Hathor is a magical rite to help women allow their attractiveness to shine forth. Men could use the young god Horus in human form and become at one with him as "God of masculine beauty and strength."

Preparations

Prior to the rite, create an image of Hathor in her horned headdress in a similar way to your Isis picture. You will also need a small amulet that you can consecrate for this rite. Anything with the image of Hathor on it would be ideal, or a simple image such as an ankh. Set up an altar with water, incense, and candles. Green is an appropriate color for Hathor as it is associated with Venus in the Western esoteric tradition. For Horus, burn gold or yellow candles. Place the deity and your amulet on the altar.

The Rite

Allow an hour and a half for the rite and your ritual bath or shower. Place your image of the goddess on the altar and light the altar candles and incense. Perform the meditative awareness exercise described in Chapter 2 (*pp. 40–1*) and then spend a few

RIGHT

While at your altar, visualize Hathor standing before you as a beautiful Egyptian woman.

A GLAMOR RITE

You will need
* an image of Hathor
* a small amulet
* a clean white cloth
* a small bowl of water
* incense and a burner
* green candles for Hathor
* gold or yellow candles for Horus

*Merge yourself with your image of Hathor
until you look out from her eyes.*

minutes gazing at the image of Hathor. Close your eyes and begin to focus on your breathing. Visualize Hathor standing in front of you in the form of a beautiful Egyptian woman. Imagine that you are approaching Hathor, who is surrounded by a warm pink glow. You move closer to the goddess and find that she is drawing you into her. Her divine femininity merges with your aura until you find yourself looking out into your room with her eyes. Say the following words aloud or to yourself:

> *I am one with the goddess Hathor,*
> *I embrace with her arms.*
> *I am the innermost essence of woman,*
> *I am the Goddess of Love:*
> *none will forget my radiance.*

When you are ready, focus on your breathing and slowly come back to wakefulness. Without breaking your concentration, take your amulet and pass it through the incense smoke. While doing this you can say the following words:

> *May the air carry this perfume to the goddess;*
> *may her power and beauty be present.*
> *Cleanse and consecrate this ankh;*
> *may it empower me with her presence.*

Take the amulet in one hand and briefly immerse it in water, saying:

> *With this symbol of Divine Life,*
> *may her power and beauty be present.*
> *Cleanse and consecrate this ankh,*
> *may it empower me with her presence.*

Hold the amulet in both hands and say three times:

> *The power of the goddess be within,*
> *the power of the goddess surround me,*
> *the power of the goddess be without.*
> *May her power and beauty be*
> *manifest for all to see.*

Be sure you wear this amulet only when you want to draw upon the glamor of Hathor.

7

Divination and Dreams

The Egyptians were firm believers in the ability to predict the future. Specialist diviners used objects, such as a reflecting pool of dark liquid, a crystal ball, the movement of the sea, or a flame, to focus, enter a light trance, and obtain information from the otherworld. An important magical role exclusive to women in Ancient Egypt was acting as a rekhet, *or "knowing one." Rekhet were renowned mediums with a special talent for communicating with the dead.*

Another way to obtain guidance was to consult an oracle—a person or image that could communicate directly with the questioner or through an intermediary. Deity statues acted as oracles. Consecrating a deity statue involved the ceremony known as "Opening the Mouth" that was used to empower a mummy. A consecrated statue contained some of the deity's essence and acted as a channel for its power. In traditional societies without modern policing methods, oracles are often used to help solve crimes. In religious festivals, Egyptian deity statues were frequently processed about town, much like Mediterranean Catholic festivals and Hindu festivals today.

LEFT
A head of the god Amun carved from quartzite, 18th dynasty,
Cairo Museum. The pharaoh was considered to be the
incarnation of Amun.

A Theft of Five Shirts

One New Year's Festival, the great Festival of Opet, when the image of the god Amun-Re was carried about the town, a security guard called Amunemwia sought help from the oracle. Amunemwia's job was to guard a nobleman's storehouse, but unfortunately Egypt's hot noonday sun had proved too much for him; he had fallen asleep and an opportunistic thief had seized his chance, breaking into the storehouse and making off with five colored shirts.

Amunemwia would have been the prime suspect and he was anxious to solve the crime. He

approached the statue of Amun and asked if the god would help him catch the thief. Oracular deities did not necessarily speak, although the darkness inside the inner sanctuaries of many temples would have allowed a priest or priestess to throw his or her voice to give the impression that this is what had occurred. Often answers were conveyed by signs. Here, the statue responded by nodding its head; presumably the carrier priests moved the statue slightly to signify assent. The names of all the townspeople were read aloud. When it came to a farmer called Pethyauemdiamun, the statue nodded. The accused farmer protested his innocence, insisting that the priests consult two other statues, but the result was still the same.

Pethyauemdiamun continued to repeatedly protest his innocence, but when he was returned to the original statue, he decided the game was up. He broke down, confessed, and offered to return the clothing that he had stolen. He received one hundred blows of a staff and was told that if he ever stole anything again he would be fed to the crocodiles. No doubt the priests of Amun were good psychologists. Few superstitious Egyptians would be able to endure the scrutiny of a group of stern-faced Amun priests.

LEFT

The façade of the temple of Hathor at Denderah, a 19th-century lithograph by David Roberts. Temples such as this would have housed priests and priestesses able to interpret visions.

Public and Private Oracles

The title *peh-netcher* may be translated as "petitioner to the god." This word describes the common Egyptian practice of receiving personal communication from a deity whose message can be interpreted by an oracle. There are two different types of oracles, the public and the private. Public oracular interpretation could be used as evidence in a court of law. Messages about matters of public interest would be announced in public in the same way that government economic predictions are made today.

Shamanic-type providers of private oracles would have existed in every Egyptian village and settlement, and they would also have provided charms and other folk magic. The best known, however, are official temple oracles. Temples had many different types of priests and priestesses. There were lector priests, who performed mundane tasks and recited the liturgy of the gods and goddesses, and there were specialists who were consulted in matters of divination. The Greeks divided these diviners into *horoskopoi* and *oneirocrites*. As the name suggests, *horoskopoi* were astrologers whose main function was to interpret horoscopes and chart the movement of the stars. *Oneirocrites* specialized in receiving oracular information from the gods through visions or dreams and they had their own consulting rooms within temples. Oracular dreaming was a common form of divination in Egypt from an early period.

Seeking Guidance from an Oracle

To perform a temple divination, a specialist oracular priest or priestess would isolate him or herself in a temple consulting room. The oracle would meditate upon the petitioner's question in darkness and silence. This sensory isolation was an essential part of the process—the stilling of the conscious mind meant that images and ideas could come to the surface. The oracle would look at a burning flame in a lamp, or at a bowl filled with dark liquid to provide a focus for the clairvoyance. The priest or priestess would have been experienced enough, through the use of breath control and meditation, to enter into a trancelike state where he or she could access the world of the divine. To help achieve visions, many shamanic cultures used, and still use, hallucinogenic plants, such as the ayahuasca vine of South America and the laurel leaves of Ancient Greece, but there is no evidence of this in Ancient Egypt. Presumably inner discipline, spiritual purity, practice, and psychic ability were considered sufficient to enable an oracle to access his or her clairvoyant powers.

Communicating with the God Anubis

Scrying involves focusing the attention on something flickering or reflective until visions appear. We know something about how this was done in Egypt through the London-Leiden Papyrus. The purpose of the papyrus is to communicate with the god Anubis. Some parts of this papyrus are fragmentary, so, in the ceremony that follows, we have reconstructed some of the text.

Anubis is the son of the goddess Nepthys, sister of Isis. He is depicted either in the form of a seated jackal or as a standing human figure with a jackal's head, carrying a staff. Anubis is a walker between the worlds of the living and the dead; he guides the spirits of the dead to judgment. As one who travels between different realms, he can assist in clairvoyance by providing information from other realms of consciousness to that of the everyday world.

The London-Leiden Papyrus describes a scrying ceremony where a child acts as the medium. Temple training could begin in Egypt at an early age. Children do not have the same inhibitions as adults about accessing the world of dream and vision; they often find it difficult to discriminate between waking and dreaming, what has happened in the material world, and what has happened in the dream world. Children's dreams are often full of wondrous beings that talk with them and it is only a small step from this world of the imagination to the strange and mystical world of the clairvoyant.

RIGHT

Anubis greeting the deceased Pharaoh Seti I, Abydos, 19th dynasty. Note the flow of ankhs that are issuing from the Djed scepter held by Anubis. These are meant to bestow life to the dead pharaoh.

The Scrying Ceremony

The instructions begin with the preparation of a scrying bowl. The bowl should be made of bronze with an image of Anubis inscribed inside it. A flat surface is covered with sand and three bricks placed on it to support the bowl. Sand symbolized a variety of things to the Ancient Egyptians. Its sterility made it a perfect purification material and it was used extensively in the foundations of temples. It was also cast before religious processions so that the bearers of the deity statue would tread upon pure sand and not the impure ground. Another papyrus recommends that sand be used as a platform for the placement of magical images. The scrying is performed from a prone position. Four blocks are laid on the sand in front of the bowl to support the scryer's body as he or she lies down in front of it. The bowl is filled with water that has been kept away from the sun. In Egypt, the moon was thought to fill an object with visionary power, but the sun only negated the effect. Oil is poured onto the water to provide a surface that reflects light. Another method is to fill the bowl with lamp oil and float a lighted wick on it. A lighted lamp is placed in front of the bowl to the right and to the left, a censer with smoking incense. Once the scryer is in position, he or she takes a cloth and pulls it over his or her head, so that only the bowl is seen. The scryer closes his or her eyes and asks for inner vision through an invocation.

SCRYING
You will need
✳ a brass, copper, or bronze bowl
✳ a purple or violet candle
✳ incense and a burner
✳ silver river sand
✳ a tray
✳ a large piece of cloth

The scryer then calls upon the god Anubis to send visions from the otherworld. When the invocation is complete, the scryer opens his or her eyes and looks in the bowl and reports whatever he or she sees. A scribe would sit close to record the symbols, visual imagery, and any words that came into the scryer's consciousness. Temple staff would interpret the imagery. At the end of the scrying, the scryer would bid farewell to Anubis, sender of visions.

Scrying for Yourself

This is a divination method that you can easily adapt for your own use. You will need to obtain a brass, copper, or bronze bowl. The image of Anubis inside is not essential but, if you would like one, rather than engraving it as the original instructions suggest, you could paint an image of Anubis inside the bowl,

CALLING FOR INNER VISION

Open my eyes, open my eyes,
open my eyes, open my eyes.
Open your eyes,
open your eyes,
open your eyes.
Open Tat, open Nap,
open Tat, open Nap
open Tat, open Nap.
Open unto me,
open unto me,
open unto me.

using a non-water-soluble paint. For the sandy surface, silver river sand is ideal. Some shops sell this for children's play pits and it can be found in DIY stores.

Perform the divination at night or in a darkened room. Before the divination exercise, have a ritual bath or shower and perform the meditative awareness exercise. Place a candle to one side of the bowl and some burning incense to the other. Rather than lying down to perform the scrying, you could place the bowl on a sand-covered tray on a table. Place a large cloth over your head and pull it forward so that you screen off your side vision and can focus on the bowl.

Before beginning, say the chant from the scrying ceremony above to open your vision and concentrate your thoughts on what you are about to do. Then call upon the god Anubis to assist you. You could visualize an image of Anubis and then chant his name using the technique described in Chapter 5 (*pp. 76–7*). You could chant either "Anubis," the Greek form of his name, or "Anpu," the Egyptian form. Now gaze at the darkened surface of the water and see what images appear. Usually they will not be pictures on the surface of the water but will appear in your mind's eye.

LEFT
Put your scrying bowl on a flat
surface and draw a cloth over your
head so that your attention is
focused on the bowl.

A Window into the Otherworld

What are the images that come into your mind during these exercises? Obviously they are images from your own unconscious, but they are a result of a heightened state of awareness in which we can become aware of more subtle impressions and insights than those normally registered by our conscious minds. By appealing to the divine to assist you, you are accessing your inner divine self that has a deeper, wider vision than your everyday personality. Our divine self has a level of awareness that can sometimes transcend the normal boundaries of time and space to give us the gift of clairvoyance.

Dreams and the Voice of the Gods

In Egypt, advice from deities such as the god Anubis could be sought by consulting an oracle or medium. The oracle would contact the deity through scrying or another trance exercise. Messages from the gods might also come unbidden through dreams. Since dreams had a sacred quality, most people would not have had the confidence to interpret their own. If a dream seemed significant and to carry an important message, or if its content was disturbing in some way, people would turn to a priest or priestess to help them, in much the same way as people turn to psychotherapists nowadays. An expert, a *shesh-per-ankh*, from the "House of Life" or temple library, would carry out the interpretations.

Dreams as Problem-Solving Devices

Doctors often used dreams as a source of medical diagnosis if an illness was too baffling for normal diagnostic methods. One medical invocation in Egyptian texts is to call for the presence of the famous doctor, Imhotep—who was proclaimed a god after his death—to appear in a dream with the answer to a particular health question. This might seem an odd way to go about solving a medical problem, but people frequently have the experience of waking up with the answer to a question that has been troubling them over a long period of time.

RIGHT
The Great Sphinx at Giza gazes enigmatically into the distance with the Pyramid of Cheops behind. A cobra originally adorned its head but this was found lying broken at its feet in the early 19th century. This is now kept in the British Museum.

A Sphinx Dream

Many important dreams are recorded in Egyptian texts. The dreams of nobles, senior officials, and Egyptian royalty, however, might have great significance. A carved stela found between the paws of the Sphinx describes how, while out hunting, Prince Tutmosis fell asleep in the shade of the Great Sphinx at Giza. The Sphinx spoke to the young prince in a dream, telling him that if he would clear away the sand that was beginning to envelop the Sphinx, he would one day become pharaoh. Tutmosis did as his dream commanded and the prophecy was fulfilled. Although his father had numerous sons, Tutmosis did become pharaoh Tutmosis IV.

Dreamtime

Each night our brains process the events of the day, storing them in our memory. Some of what is processed is aspects of events and encounters that we have not noticed at the time. Our conscious minds cannot take notice of absolutely everything that is happening at any given moment. This does not mean that other sensory impressions are lost, simply that we have not had time to attend to them.

Recalling Dreams

To recall a dream, you must record it as soon as you wake up. It is important to keep a pen and paper beside your bed so you can record your dreams before you talk to anyone. As soon as you start thinking about other things, you will begin to lose the memory of your dream. Some people protest that they never remember their dreams but once you have broken through into your dream life, you will find you will be able to recall them easily.

To have a deep and dream-filled sleep, it is important to relax before going to bed. Do not watch television immediately beforehand; instead, light some scented candles in your bedroom and play some relaxing music. Herbal pillows can help produce a relaxing sleep; lavender, for example, is an herb that stimulates the psyche. Stores that sell herbs can also recommend teas and herbal mixtures for pillows that will help you to remember dreams.

Anubis

The jackal-headed god performs two important ritual functions when dealing with death and the afterlife. He is an overseer of the weighing of the heart of the deceased and he is also the one who performs the ceremony of the "Opening of the Mouth." Whether you believe in the literal reality of the god Anubis is not important. Anubis is a symbol of a deity who can enter into different states of consciousness and who

has been invoked for millennia for just this purpose. Powerful symbols that have been used in spiritual work over generations can cause a strong response in our unconscious minds. Stores that sell Egyptian statues will have statues of Anubis and you might like to buy one to put in your bedroom.

The Meaning of your Dreams

To analyze your dreams, look for recurring patterns and themes. Dream symbols are individual. They will mean one thing in the context of one person's life, relationships, and personality and something quite different to someone else. Not all dreams will be significant, but we can usually sense when a dream is trying to tell us something important.

We frequently dream about unfinished business—everything from unsolved crossword puzzles, to tasks

LEFT
Lavender is an herb that can stimulate dreaming.

A wooden shrine to the recumbent Anubis, gilded in gold leaf as part of the treasure trove from the tomb of Tutankhamun. Anubis is present as protector of the King's resting place and custodian of the afterlife.

we may not have had time to complete at work, to personal problems. If we can remember our dreams, we can be enriched by all manner of insights that normally escape our notice. Accessing and recording our dreams will give us important insights but we can go farther. One technique that is used in modern psychotherapy, as well as in ancient magical traditions, is to enter into dialogue with the figures that appear in our dreams. This is a technique that Jungian psychologists call "active imagination." If we dream of a co-worker, it might mean that we are really dreaming about that person, or it might mean that we recognize some quality in him or her that it is important for us to acknowledge in ourselves. To find out more, imagine yourself back in the dream scenario and ask the person: why have you come; what are you trying to tell me? In other words, enter into a conversation with the dream image. This works not only with people but also with inanimate objects. The dream world is like a shamanic universe—we can assume that everything in it has its own consciousness.

8

Figures and Images in Egyptian Magic

Egyptian magic frequently used human figurines known as ushabti, *molded or sculpted from clay, wax, or dough. Ushabti are in the form of standing mummies, sometimes with their own model coffin. Ushabti are magically empowered sculptures imbued with life.*

The tombs of rich nobles often contain ushabti servants equipped with useful items, such as digging tools. The otherworld was thought to be much like this one; there would be work to do, things to organize, canals to excavate, and parties to attend. Not surprisingly, people who had not engaged in manual labor in this world were anxious not to do so in the next. The solution was an ushabti, a personal "gofer." As a symbol of ownership the deceased's name was cut or painted upon the ushabti together with a useful spell, such as: "In the event of my being condemned to spread dust on the fields of the otherworld, or to fill the channels with water, such work shall be performed for me by them [the ushabti] and no obstacle to doing so shall be put in the way." Once the spell is spoken, the ushabti is meant to call out, "Here I am to whoever calls me," and it completes the tasks.

LEFT
Two painted wooden ushabti, 20th dynasty. These figurines often had their own decorated box to live in.

Making a Ushabti

You can create your own magical figurine, similar to the ushabti. In this case, your servant is not performing manual labor in the afterlife, but will act as an intermediary between the realm of the spirit and the world of matter. To consecrate the ushabti, you will need a small ankh to place inside it. You can buy an ankh from a store, or you could make your own. Use the ceremony at the end of Chapter 3 (*pp. 52–3*) to bless the ankh. Wear it next to your skin for a month, so that it forms an etheric link with you that can be transferred direct to the ushabti.

MAKING A USHABTI

You will need

✳ a small ankh

✳ your picture of Isis

✳ wax or clay to model with

✳ a heatproof bowl

✳ a saucepan

✳ a metal spatula or knife

✳ a clean white cloth

✳ a large bowl of water

✳ incense and a burner

✳ two altar candles

✳ one red candle

✳ a small bowl of milk

ABOVE
Maintain your meditative state while modeling your ushabti.

RIGHT
Limestone figurine of a female brewer, c. 2325 BCE, Egyptian Museum, Cairo. This would be placed in a tomb to ensure ready supplies of beer in the afterlife. The Egyptians wished to enjoy themselves in death as much as they had in life.

Modeling Materials

Wax can be obtained by melting down candles. Place a heatproof bowl in a pan of boiling water. About eight candles 1 in. thick and 6 in. high should provide sufficient wax. Cut small pieces of wax into the bowl with a knife; keep adding pieces of wax until all the wax has melted. Remove the bowl from the pan and allow it to cool. When it is cool enough to pick up, take it to your altar. You need it to be soft but not set. Clay can be molded in the hands until it is soft.

Ritual Preparation

The rite is best performed at night. Allow three hours for your first attempt. Clean your sacred space and set up an altar as described at the end of Chapter 4 (*pp. 66–7*). Place your picture or statue of Isis on the altar, together with a bowl of water large enough to immerse your ushabti in, incense, two altar candles, and a red candle to symbolize life energy. New age shops often sell Egyptian incenses. You should also have a small bowl of milk. This represents life-giving sustenance and is for the symbolic feeding of the ushabti. You will also need your modeling material and your knife or spatula to make your ushabti. Have a ritual bath or shower.

Modeling the Ushabti

Prepare your modeling material and work it into an oblong about 6 in. long. Light your candles and incense and dim any other lights. You might like to play some soft music. Perform the meditative awareness exercise at the end of Chapter 2 (*pp. 40–1*). Then, sitting before the altar, take the oblong and begin molding or carving the figurine. Be conscious that you are giving of yourself to the ushabti while doing this. Now mold a figure that looks like a mummy. Allow this to harden. Leave a hollow in the back where your ankh can be inserted and keep a plug of material to cover this later on. Check that the ushabti can stand without support. If not, mold a base for the feet, so that the weight distribution is correct. Once you have completed your ushabti, place it on the altar.

Sanctifying your Sacred Space

Consecrate and cense your sacred space by circuiting the altar clockwise. Take your water bowl and, starting from the back of your altar, walk clockwise in a complete circuit around it, sprinkling water on the ground as you go. You can use these words of blessing as you walk:

> O great gods and gentle goddesses of the land of Khemet. I make this offering of water to prepare a temple for your worship. May this circle be a barrier that no evil presence or thought can break. I do this in the name of Maat. May my voice and intention be true and my heart pure.

Return the water bowl to the altar and process with your incense burner around the altar as before, holding it up to allow the incense smoke to consecrate your sacred space, and saying:

> O great gods and gentle goddesses of the land of Khemet. I make this offering of incense to prepare a temple for your worship. May this circle be a barrier that no evil presence or thought can break. I do this in the name of Maat. May my voice and intention be true and my heart pure.

Return the incense burner to the altar. Stand in front of your altar and open your arms out at shoulder height, your palms facing the altar, and ask the blessing of the gods:

> I perform this rite in the names of the Ennead of On:
> Atum-Re, Shu, Tefnut, Nuit, Geb,
> Isis, Osiris, Nepthys, and Set.
> May they and their heirs:
> Horus, Bast, Anubis, and the Sons of Horus,
> be favorable unto me.
> May my Divine Father Geb be my foundation;
> may he be strong beneath my feet.
> May my Divine Mother Nuit be my protection;
> may the arch of her body shelter the universe.

Look at your ushabti and channel your energy toward it in the same way as you performed the consecration of your amulet in Chapter 3 (*pp. 52–3*). Imagine that your spine is an energized column of light—the Djed column of the god Osiris. Allow the column of light to reach higher and higher above you until it stretches to the heavens. Allow the column of energy to reach deep into the earth from the base of your spine. Let the power in your spine build up and flow outward across your back and down into your arms. The light that is flowing from your spine is energizing your arms and hands. Now take the ushabti and allow energy from your hands to flow into it, energizing it. When you are finished, kneel before the altar and raise the figure above your head in both hands as you recite the following words:

> *O Great Gods and Goddesses of Creation,*
> *gaze favorably upon this image,*
> *that it may serve as a messenger*
> *between this world*
> *and the realm of the divine.*
> *Thrice great Thoth and thrice again your power!*
> *Give me your Heka to assist in creation;*
> *to travel between this world*
> *and the realm of the gods.*

Concentrate on opening up a channel between yourself, grounded to the earth, and the gods above in the night sky. The figurine is suspended in the void between. Draw your power, through your arms, into the figurine and use the image of a spinning potter's wheel to work your way into a light trance. When you feel the figurine has been sufficiently blessed, immerse it in the basin of water, saying:

> *As the Nile sustains and gives life,*
> *so does the water of life give and sustain the*
> *power of becoming.*
> *Give life to this ushabti, so it may serve as a*
> *messenger between me and the gods.*

LEFT
Circumambulation, or walking in a circular manner for ritual, was an important aspect of Egyptian magical practice.

Awakening the Ushabti

Remove the figurine and hold it over the incense smoke, saying:

*As the Divine breath of the gods sustains
and gives life, so does this incense give
and sustain the power of Being. Give life to this
ushabti, so it may serve as a messenger between
me and the gods.*

Holding the ushabti in one hand, dip a fingertip of the other hand into the milk. Anoint the head, breast, and feet of the ushabti with the milk, saying:

*Great Divine One, Hathor, Mother of the Gods,
as your divine milk sustains and gives life, so does
this milk give and sustain the power of enduring.
Give life to this, my ushabti, so it may serve
as a messenger between me and the gods.*

Now insert the ankh into the space in the back of the ushabti. Place a plug of material over it and smooth it over. If you are using wax, heat a metal knife or spatula in a candle flame and melt the edges of the wax plug so they merge with the wax of the ushabti's back. If you are using clay, use the water on your altar to moisten the clay to stick the plug to the ushabti. The plug of material does not have to cover the ankh completely but it should hold it in firmly. Stand the ushabti facing you on the altar and speak to it, saying the following:

*Thus are the sacred words spoken by the god Osiris:
"O ushabti of mine, I call upon you to assist me,
you shall stand before me saying: 'Here am I to do
your bidding.' May whatever I ask of you be in
accordance with the will of the Divine, bringing harm
to no one. Travel to the realm of the Duat and bring
forth to me whatever knowledge I desire. Be a friend
and companion until such time as I put you to rest."*

Extinguish your candles and return to the everyday world as we described in the exercise at the end of Chapter 2 (*pp. 40–1*).

Using the Ushabti

There are many ways to use the ushabti. If you want to obtain information in a dream—such as the whereabouts of something you have lost—place the ushabti near your bed. Light a candle and ask the ushabti to send you inspiration in your dreams. Extinguish the candle and go to bed. You can also ask for the assistance of the ushabti whenever you need creative inspiration. When you are not using

the ushabti, it should be wrapped in a cloth, placed in a box, and kept in a private drawer or cupboard.

When you no longer need your ushabti any more, it should be laid to rest by burying it in the earth where it will not be disturbed. Place it in a hole and say these words of departure:

O ushabti of mine, I thank you,
for the time you have served me,
faithfully and true.
Your period of service has come to an end
and you can sleep deep within
the nourishing earth.
Great is the power of the gods,
and greater still the power
that moves the universe.
Thrice great Thoth and
thrice still great,
I thank you for your blessing.

Now cover the ushabti completely with earth and stamp down the surface, making sure that this hiding place is not obvious to anyone else. Keep it safe and undisturbed until you next need a guide for your unconscious mind.

LEFT
Consecrate your figurine
with incense and milk.

9

Health and Healing

Ancient Egyptians had an international reputation as healers and sages. Rich people in neighboring states wanted the best medical treatment money could buy, so only an Egyptian doctor would do.

The closest word to doctor in Egyptian is swnw, *possibly pronounced "soo-noo," for a male doctor, and for a female doctor,* swnwt, *or "soo-noot." The same word can be used to describe a priest involved in embalming the dead. Others were acknowledged as* wer swnu, *or "great" doctors, perhaps the equivalent of our hospital consultants today.*

When medical knowledge became more complex and the populations became more concentrated in cities, doctors began to specialize. Numerous different practitioners of the healing arts evolved. Eventually, medicine had its own administrators, controllers, and inspectors. The accounts of Greek visitors to Egypt describe doctors who specialized in the abdomen (gastroenterology), the eyes (ophthalmology), or trauma such as broken bones. Medical knowledge was recorded in textbooks such as the Ebers Papyrus, written around 3,500 years ago, in the ninth year of the reign of pharaoh Amenhotep I.

LEFT
A priest in a distinctive leopard-skin cape pouring libations to the sun god, 1186–1069 BCE, in the Egyptian Museum, Cairo. Priests could act as healing intermediaries between the world of the living and that of the gods.

Magic and Medicine

In the ancient world, magic and medicine were inseparable. The Egyptian physician's skill was based on an intimate knowledge and learned use of plants, minerals, and animals that had pharmacological effects recognized by medicine today. However, the accompanying spells, incantations, and chants, coupled with the proper ritual gestures, were considered to be equally important, as well as the physician's spiritual links with healing deities such as Thoth.

RIGHT

A section from the Ebers Papyrus, one of the most important medical texts of Ancient Egypt.

Many Ancient Egyptian spells and incantations survive, thanks to papyrus being preserved by the arid Egyptian climate. Most are an integral part of religious observance, particularly funeral rites. The largest collection of spells and magical instructions comes from the Pyramid Texts and the Coffin Texts. Together, these are known as the *Book of the Dead* or, to give a better translation, the *Book of Going Forth by Day*. Other spells and incantations were acts of ritual magic by established professionals—the high priests of various state-sanctioned cults. Other spells were the tools of healers and other professionals.

Medical Spells

Some documents were medical texts that contained a combination of medical techniques, spells, invocations to healing deities, and methods for exorcizing demons. The Egyptian verb for exorcize was *sitcher*, which means "to cause to fall." A common explanation for disease was spirit possession, so a healer's ability to use words of power to banish demons was important. On a more specific level, the Ebers Papyrus describes how to treat burns. The healer first makes a mixture to anoint the burns, made from the breast milk of a woman who has borne a male child, gum, and ram's hair. The milk and gum resin formula would have had a practical soothing effect as the burn healed. While putting the mixture on the wounds, the healer sought divine help by invoking the goddess Isis and asking her to treat the patient as her own son Horus. "Your son Horus is burned in the desert. Is there any water there? There is no water. I have water in my mouth and the Nile between my thighs. I have come to extinguish the fire." The reference to water had two purposes. On a practical level, water is a purifying and cleansing liquid. On a symbolic level, water extinguishes fire. Through sympathetic magic, the reference to water is to alleviate the pain and discomfort of the burned skin. The healer is also drawing upon his or her own inner power through the watery element present in the body—in this case spittle and urine, the "water in the mouth" and "Nile between my thighs." Both urine and spittle were considered powerful agents of magic. Urine has many healing and sterilizing properties and is still used in Western herbalism and Ayurvedic medicine.

Exorcism

Most early medical traditions believed that illness could have spiritual as well as physical causes. If Egyptian doctors believed an illness was caused by malicious spirits or through someone ill-wishing the patient or casting a spell on them, the disease would be exorcized and spells would be used to draw out the offending spirit. Exorcism is still used as a treatment by some Christians and Muslims, and in shamanic societies, such as those of the Amazon.

Spiritual Healing

Academic books on Egyptian magic are increasingly aware of the necessity of defining terms such as magic, spells, and incantations as the Ancient Egyptians would have viewed them. In the past, scholars often brought a rational perspective into their analysis that could be both condescending and misleading. This attitude looked at magic as a kind of primitive science: when a pharmaceutical drug or surgical technique was not available then people resorted to spells and incantations. This misses the point and ignores the influence of the mind on the body. In Egyptian healing, a herbal treatment with pharmacological properties was boosted by the wearing of an amulet, or the recitation of a particular spell. The ingredients might not have been successful alone, but combined holistically they might have brought about the desired effect of a return to good health.

Mind Over Matter

Other spells have little direct medicinal value and work through what is known as "contagious magic." In this type of spell, power is transmitted from one object to another through physical contact. A popular Egyptian healing technique involving contagious magic was to write a healing spell on parchment in water-soluble ink. Water was poured over the parchment and the ink run off into a container. The water was then given to the patient so that he or she could drink the magic of the words. This might seem unlikely to help, but the power of the mind in boosting the body's healing defenses was understood much better by the ancients than by scientific Western medicine, although this is now beginning to change. If the patient believed in the efficacy of the magical water, then this could make a difference. In the absence of any alternative treatments, it seemed quite logical to try it.

Scientific research has shown that if we have confidence in the treatment we are receiving, and in the physician or surgeon responsible for that treatment, we heal

LEFT
*A standing sculpture of
Sekhmet, lion-headed goddess
of war and healing.*

more quickly. If we are relaxed, the body's autoimmune system is more robust and can fight disease and heal wounds much more efficiently. Egyptian healing magic helped to boost the patient's confidence and this would therefore improve the efficacy of the medical treatment. Spiritual or magical healing may go beyond an individual's belief in the treatment, however. There is both scientific evidence and documentary records of patients being healed successfully when they have no idea they are being helped and are not even physically present. Christians and Muslims explain absent healing as the intervention of God or Allah. An indigenous tribal shaman would credit it to his spirit helpers and power animals, and a modern healing therapist might well locate the source of the transformation in the as yet little understood interventions of the human unconscious.

Sekhmet

Healing that cures the patient by using spiritual energy generated by the healer is common today. The Ancient Egyptians also practiced this type of healing. The Ebers Papyrus describes healers of the temple of the lioness-headed goddess Sekhmet performing spiritual healing. Sekhmet is a fearsome goddess who was associated with both war and healing: Sekhmet's priests and priestesses were considered particularly adept at the healing arts. Pharaohs seeking to defend Egypt, as well as those who wanted to drive out all

ABOVE
Statues of Sekhmet are found standing or seated on a throne. This enthroned Sekhmet is from Medinet Habu, Thebes, Egypt.

kinds of pestilence and disease, would invoke Sekhmet. Sekhmet's wrath was terrible. At one point she nearly destroyed humanity in a rage when people failed to worship the god Re properly. She is depicted standing with a lotus-headed staff in one hand and an ankh in the other, or seated on a throne.

Herbal Medicine

Many kinds of medical treatments were available in Ancient Egypt, but the most popular was herbal medicine, boosted, of course, by magic. Egyptian herbal medicine used deductive and analytical experimentation alongside magic and incantations, and its efficacy has just begun to be recognized in modern science. For a long time the instructions to pick herbs at certain times of the day, moon phase, or season—before dawn or during a full moon, for example—were dismissed as superstition. However, scientific research shows that certain alkaloids or chemicals are present in plants in greater numbers before sunrise, but decrease as the day grows brighter. So, this system of treatment can be seen to have a scientific, as well as a magical, background.

ABOVE

Thyme was used for medicinal purposes and to flavor food.

Herbs used by the Egyptians

Thyme, a popular culinary herb, is often unappreciated these days for its medicinal properties, but it does appear in a number of herbals. The Egyptians called it *tai-iti* and used it as an antiseptic and a preservative. Thyme is an important ingredient in modern embalming fluid and may have been part of the mysterious oils and herbal infusions used for that purpose by the Ancient Egyptians. Thyme is reputed to have an invigorating effect and to cure headaches, although these uses were not noted in surviving Egyptian texts. The Egyptians did note, however, that the plant helps clear phlegm and release wind.

Willow bark has astringent properties that were widely recognized in the ancient world. Salicyl is the active chemical that provides the essential antiseptic ingredient. Willow appears frequently in tomb art and we know that other contemporary peoples, such as the Greeks and Romans, used willow to dress wounds, reduce inflammation, and relieve pain.

Cannabis sativa, or hemp, was known as *shemsemet* in Ancient Egyptian. Hemp has many useful properties: its fibers are used for making rope and it has many medical uses that are being rediscovered. Today cannabis has been found to alleviate the symptoms of multiple sclerosis and is used to treat glaucoma. For this, the Egyptians ground celery and cannabis into a powder and left it out overnight to soak in the dew. The patient's eyes were washed in the mixture.

A deceased man and his wife approach an offering table laden with food. A lotus adorns the perfumed cone of fat on the wife's head.

Mandragora officinarum, or mandrake, was probably introduced into Egypt at about the time of the New Kingdom. Its conspicuous shape and greenish yellow or purple flowers began to appear in tomb and temple art as part of floral garlands, growing in ornamental gardens, or being held in the hands of the people depicted therein. The mandrake plant is very versatile and the flowers, leaves, and root can all be used in medicine; the Egyptians certainly made the most of this plant's extraordinary properties. The root has a narcotic effect and both modern herbalists and Egyptian healers prescribe juice from its root as a painkiller and sleeping potion; the leaves were used externally for ulcers. It was also used to treat wounds and toothache.

The two species of lotus that are native to Egypt are the blue and white water lilies. In addition to being beautiful plants in their own right, with blooms that cover ponds and lakes, the lotus was also very important in Egyptian medical preparations. Both species contain narcotic alkaloids, but the blue lotus, *Nymphaea caerulea,* known in Egyptian as *seshhen,* is of the greatest medical interest. It was used to treat constipation, hair loss, and jaundice. The Greek chronicler Discorides defined the lotus as a "cooling herb" and noted its effectiveness when a fevered patient was placed in a bath containing lotus flowers.

Blue lotus was also used as a recreational drug and features frequently in banquet and party scenes found in tomb art. Even drinking a small amount dissolved in alcohol produces feelings of euphoria and general well-being. With the lotus being viewed as a symbol of love and beauty, it is unsurprising to see it listed in Egyptian manuals of magic as a powerful and often-used aphrodisiac.

Both beautiful and useful, the white lotus was a valuable addition to the Egyptian doctor's medicine chest.

Invoking Healing Deities

To increase the effectiveness of herbal remedies, deities were invoked to empower the herbs. Part of the process of healing would be for both physician and patient to appeal to these deities for assistance. If the physician was a devotee of Thoth, for instance, the first thing he would do was invoke the name of Thoth, to draw down the power, or Heka, of the god within himself and transfer it to the patient. At that moment, the healer would be divinely associated with the god and possessed of his special magical power. He would then proceed with an examination, diagnosis, and treatment.

Different deities had their own specialisms. The head of the goddess Selket, or Serqet, was adorned with a scorpion. Her worship is of great antiquity and, alongside Hathor and Neith, the desert goddess is among the oldest in the Nile valley. The sting from a scorpion or a snake bite would have been one of the leading causes of death and illness in Ancient Egypt, especially among children. A strong goddess was needed to protect children from stings and bites and also to draw the poison out and cure the person. Selket was used to both ward off attack and cure the afflicted.

Thoth, Lord of Physicians and Greatest Magician

Thoth was a talented god and patron of magicians, scribes, and physicians. He is also credited with inventing aspects of civilized life: a calendar, social order, and hieroglyphs. As the deity responsible for the invention of the calendar, Thoth gave his name to the first month of the Egyptian year. The first calendars in most civilizations were lunar rather than solar because changes in the lunar

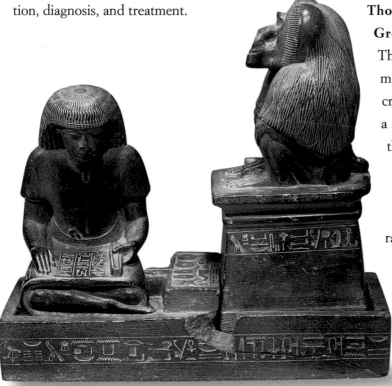

LEFT
The royal scribe Nebmerutef writing under the protection of the god Thoth in ape form. Thoth was considered to be the inventor of the hieroglyph and was therefore patron of scribes. New Kingdom, 18th dynasty, c. 1390–1352 BCE.

month were easier to note and record. Thoth is seen as the personification of the moon itself and as guardian or protector of it. He wears a headdress consisting of a full moon supported by a crescent moon.

Thoth is one of the oldest deities in the Nile valley. There are frequent references in texts from the Old Kingdom to the Feast of Thoth. Like the Horus falcon, the sacred ibis of Thoth is represented in the earliest slate palettes found in Egypt from the era before the pharaohs. The curved beak of this bird was associated with the crescent moon and its white and black feathers with the moon's waxing and waning. During the time of Narmer, one of the earliest pharaohs, a carving representing a shrine of Thoth appeared at Hierakonpolis, the royal capital. In the oldest texts, Thoth is represented by an ibis on a perch and written forms of his name are rare. In the Middle Kingdom, his name is spelled Djeheuty; later, the name appears as Tahuti, and this has evolved in modern Coptic to Thaheut. However, we are more familiar with the Greek form of the name—Thoth.

Thoth is also associated with the baboon, although the presence of baboons would have been restricted to the further reaches of Upper Egypt. This

most intelligent of animals would have been a leading contender as a symbol for the god of learning. The behavior of baboons at dawn would have also been seen as an important factor. Dawn heralds the beginning of the day for most primates and when it appears, the entire troupe is seen throwing their arms into the air in a gesture the Egyptians were to regard as a greeting or act of supplication to the sun god Re.

The Eye of Thoth

As well as becoming at one with Osiris-Orion, dead pharaohs were considered to become at one with the sun god Re during the day and with Thoth the moon during the night. In this way, they can continue to watch over and guard their people in death as in life. The left eye, the moon or eye of Thoth, is also credited with being all knowing. A 12th-dynasty inscription in the Cairo Museum speaks of Thoth as the "god who is in men's hearts: his eye examines the hearts of all." This suggests that night-time was considered to be a period of self-reflection.

God of Magic

As the most learned of the gods, Thoth became the god of magic. The two functions of intelligence and *gnosis*, or hidden knowledge, were inseparable in the Egyptian mind. This is borne out by an examination of the numerous titles ascribed to Thoth, in particular, "Great in Magic" and "Learned in Magic." The term Heka has already been described in Chapter 3 (*p. 43*) and Thoth was the deity invoked to practice it. He was dreaded by demons and caused illness to flee; he was the creator of amulets and nothing living or dead could withstand the power of his words; he was the magical protector of gods and of human beings. Whenever Thoth is depicted standing beside someone in art, he is there to intensify the individual's power and to weaken the power of his or her enemies.

Books of Thoth

From the beginning of Egyptian history, there are numerous references to books of Thoth, or manuals of magical wisdom and instruction. All magical manuals were considered mere extracts from the great *Book of Thoth*, a mythical text that was the equivalent of the Philosopher's Stone, the lost Ark of the Covenant, or the Holy Grail. It was a magical treasure that was the fount of all wisdom. Like the Grail, the *Book of Thoth* was eagerly sought after by those wanting magical or spiritual power.

In later texts Thoth is referred to as "Thrice Greatest" or "Trismegistos." The Greek writer

RIGHT
Thoth, the ibis-headed god of magic, depicted in his glory in a tomb painting. He was the most learned and powerful of the Egyptian deities.

Plutarch refers to Thoth as "many times great, we are wont to call thrice." The great Egyptologist Gaston Maspero, in his translation of the epic tale of the magician Prince Setna, gives an even more significant epithet: "Thoth the nine times great." It is probable that the threefold aspect of Thoth corresponded to the three phases of the moon, since Thoth is above all a lunar deity.

Hermapolis Magna

Thoth's principal cult center was Hemeneu, the City of the Eight, in the Hare *nome*, or administrative district, in Upper Egypt. An entire quarter of the city was presided over by the god and a large temple has recently been excavated there. It is now the modern city of el-Ashmunein. This is not to be confused with the other sacred city of Thoth, Hermopolis Parva, in the Delta.

The Greeks called the city of Hemeneu, Hermopolis Magna or "Great City of Hermes" and equated Thoth with Hermes, their own god of magic and learning. Hermes was often depicted as a winged messenger carrying a staff intertwined with two snakes. Magical knowledge was closely associated with medical knowledge among the Greeks as well as the Egyptians and Hermes' staff is the symbol of many doctors' associations around the world. In the Nubian temple of Dendur, at Philae in Aswan—and elsewhere—Thoth as physician and healer is shown by an image of the god clutching the serpent staff of medicine. In later periods, Thoth, like Imhotep the deified physician, was equated with Asclepius, a famous Greek doctor, who was later made a god. Asclepius' temple on the Greek island of Kos draws thousands of visitors each year.

RIGHT
The ibis was another of Thoth's symbols.
Its long curved beak was reminiscent
of the crescent moon.

Combined Healing

The Ancient Egyptians practiced many techniques of healing that combined what we would call conventional medical science with complementary therapies. Today, we are again acknowledging that our inner mental state has enormous impact on physical healing processes. This does not mean that magic can replace modern medicine but, in the 19th and 20th centuries, we did neglect the role that our inner psychological and spiritual state could have on healing. The combination of scientific medical practice and complementary medicine is the way forward in the 21st century and more medical practitioners are beginning to acknowledge this. Even those healing practices that some would call superstitious have a profound effect on the mind and body. "Miracles" still happen at healing shrines such as Lourdes, spiritual healing sanctuaries, and in shamanic cultures, when the patient accesses the power of the divine and his or her belief in the effectiveness of the treatment. However, there are also many charlatans who make wild claims about

LEFT
A ceremony showing the purification of two mummies from the tomb of the priest Merymaat, 18th dynasty.

their healing abilities and anybody who has any sort of medical problem should always go to a licensed and respected healer. Many countries have societies that rigorously check their members.

A Healing Technique

If you would like to try doing some similar healing, one technique you can use is a synthesis between one well-established method of distance healing and the power behind Egyptian symbolism and ritual belief. You will need to visualize an image of the person to whom you are directing the healing. A photograph, along with an object belonging to the person, is helpful, especially if you do not know the individual personally.

Healing rites involve calling upon the divine to assist in bringing about the healing. This version of the rite is addressed to Isis. After the Roman conquest of Egypt, many Romans adopted Isis as their goddess. Throughout the Roman world, the *iseums,* or temples devoted to Isis, were centers of healing and the precursor to our modern hospitals. Dedicated priestesses wearing black and white robes tended to the sick, in much the same way as religious sisters in Catholic orders did in later centuries. During the ritual, you identify yourself with the goddess Isis, so that it is not you as an individual who performs the healing, but rather the goddess Isis herself. If you prefer to identify with a male deity, you could invoke Thoth.

ABOVE
This 19th-century lithograph by David Roberts depicts the temple of Isis at Philae.

A HEALING CEREMONY

You will need

* a bowl of water
* incense and a burner
* your picture of Isis
* two small altar candles
* one blue candle
* one orange candle
* a photograph of or an object belonging to the person whom you wish to heal

Creating a Sacred Space

The first step is to clean your sacred space and set up a ritual altar. Allow an hour and a half for the rite and your ritual bath or shower. For your altar you will need a bowl of water, incense, your picture of Isis or a statue of Isis, and two small altar candles. You might like to obtain a statue of Thoth. You will also need two other candles and candlesticks, one blue and one orange. In the Western esoteric tradition, orange is the color for Thoth; blue is the color for Isis and it is often associated with healing. Place your deity image at the center of the back of the altar, with your orange candle to the right and below the deity image, making a right bottom corner of a triangle with Isis at the apex. Now place your blue candle opposite on the left-hand side of the altar, so that the Isis image and the two candles create an equal-sided triangle. Place a photograph or object from the patient in the center of the triangle. These provide a mental image and a link with the person who needs help. Consecrate your sacred space with water and incense as before. You can use the words of the ushabti ritual at the end of Chapter 8 (*pp. 104–5*).

Visualizing your Patient

The next step is to sit comfortably and enter a meditative state. Form a clear image of the person in your mind and focus precisely on the location of the medical problem. Maintain your visualization and say an Isis chant softly or silently. This chant is adapted from a healing spell in the Chester Beatty Papyrus:

It is not I who come before you,
it is the goddess Isis who approaches you;
it is the power of Isis that will heal you;
poisons of sickness depart from [now insert the name of the patient];
for it is the goddess Isis who commands you.
For I am She.
For I am.

Repeat this three times while visualizing the person you are healing. If you want to invoke Thoth, adapt the invocation to his name instead. Without breaking your concentration or focus, slowly stretch your arms out in front of you, with your hands raised and palms open, toward the photograph in the center of your triangle. Using the same technique described in the ritual of the ushabti in Chapter 8 (*pp. 104–5*), feel a blazing blue energy flow from your spinal column, through your arms and out of your fingertips. Imagine you are laying your hands on the diseased organ or part of the body; blue healing energy is flowing through you into the person you are healing. As energy flows toward the patient, visualize him or her growing more healthy. As you project energy, it is important that you replenish your own. Every few moments, focus on the link between the energy in your spine and that in the heavens and the earth.

Closing your Ritual

When it feels right, gently withdraw your energy from the person you are healing. Allow the flow of energy down your arms to cease and visualize him or her surrounded by glowing healing energy. Now allow the visualization to fade and become aware of your surroundings. You could say: "I thank the great gods and goddesses of Khemet for attending my ritual of healing. Now depart to your wonderful and starry realms in love and peace." Extinguish your candles and, if possible, leave the altar set up overnight.

RIGHT

Imagine energy flowing down your arms to reach out to the one you are healing.

Learning More

If reading this book has made you want to learn more about Ancient Egypt, here are some books that can help you explore this fascinating civilization further.

Allen, Thomas George, *The Book of the Dead or Going Forth by Day*, University of Chicago Press, 1974.

Barton, Tamsyn, *Ancient Astrology*, Routledge, 1994.

Bauval, Robert and Gilbert, Adrian, *The Orion Mystery*, BCA, 1994.

Brier, Bob, *Ancient Egyptian Magic*, Quill Publications, 1980.

Faulkner, R.O., *The Egyptian Book of the Dead (Papyrus of Ani): The Book of Going Forth By Day*, Chronicle Books, 1994.

Gardiner, Sir Alan, *Egyptian Grammar*, Oxford University Press, 1927.

Hart, George, *A Dictionary of Egyptian Gods and Goddesses*, Routledge, 1986.

Kemp, Barry J., *Ancient Egypt—Anatomy of a Civilisation*, Routledge, 1991.

Lurker, Manfred, *An Illustrated Dictionary of the Gods and Symbols of Ancient Egypt*, Thames & Hudson, 1974.

Manniche, Lise, *An Ancient Egyptian Herbal*, British Museum Press, 1991.

Nunn, John F., *Ancient Egyptian Medicine*, British Museum Press, 1996.

Pinch, Geraldine, *Magic in Ancient Egypt*, British Museum Press, 1994.

Quirke, S., *Ancient Egyptian Religion*, British Museum Press, 1992.

Rosalind, M. and Janssen, Jac J., *Growing up in Ancient Egypt*, Rubicon Press, 1996.

Strouhal, Eugen, *Life in Ancient Egypt*, Cambridge University Press, 1992.

Tyldesley, Joyce, *Daughters of Isis: Women of Ancient Egypt*, Penguin Books, 1995.

Watterson, Barbara, *The House of Horus at Edfu, Ritual in an Ancient Egyptian Temple*, Tempus, 1998.

ISIS

If you are drawn to the goddess Isis, the Fellowship of Isis is an international network for all who recognize the feminine aspect in divinity. Membership is free. Further details can be obtained from The Fellowship of Isis, Clonegal Castle, Enniscorthy, County Wexford, Ireland. To train to be a priestess or priest, write to: The Secretary, PO Box 196, London WC1A 1LY, UK.

MUSEUMS TO VISIT

The Cairo Museum, 11556 Midan el-Tahrir, Misr al-Kahira, Cairo. This undoubtedly has the largest and best collection of artifacts and monumental sculpture in the world. It also contains the treasures discovered at the tomb of Tutankhamun and the collection of royal mummies, including Rameses II. A fine modern muscum is in Luxor on Cornish Street, al-Uksur. In Alexandria, there is a lovely museum devoted to Greco-Roman Antiquities on Museum Street, 21521 Alexandria.

United States and Canada

California: Phoebe Hearst Museum of Anthropology, 103 Kroeber Hall No. 3712, University of California, Berkeley 94720–3712.
Illinois: Oriental Institute Museum, University of Chicago, 1155 East 58th Street, Chicago 60637.
Massachusetts: Museum of Fine Arts, 465 Huntington Avenue, Boston 02115.
New York: The Metropolitan Museum of Art, 5th Avenue at 82nd Street, New York 10028.
Ohio: Cleveland Museum of Art, 11150 East Boulevard, Cleveland 44106.
Pennsylvania: University of Pennsylvania Museum of Archaeoleogy and Anthropology, 33rd and Spruce Streets, Philadelphia 19104 6324.

Canada: Royal Ontario Museum, PO Box 71117, Toronto, Ontario M55 2C6.

Europe

The British Museum, Great Russell Street, London WC1B 3DG. The newly refurbished upper galleries are truly amazing; the museum also houses the Papyrus of Ani, which contains prayers and invocations that you have seen in this book; the Rosetta Stone, which first enabled people to translate the hieroglyphs; deity statues; and wall paintings from the tomb of Nebamun. The Ashmolean Museum of Art and Archaeology, Beaumont Street, Oxford OX1 2PH, is smaller than the British Museum but is stocked with extraordinary and unique artifacts. Other museums in England include The Petrie Museum of Egyptian Archeology, University College, Gower Street, London WC1E 6BT, and The Fitzwilliam Museum, Trumpington Street, Cambridge CB2 1RB. Museums elsewhere in Europe include:
Belgium: Musées Royaux d'Art et d'Histoire, Parc du Cinquantenaire 10, 1000 Bruxelles, Belgium.
France: Musée de l'Art Egyptien, Palais Universitaire, 67000 Strasbourg; Musée du Louvre, 34–36 Quai du Louvre, 75058 Paris.
Germany: Ägyptisches Museum und Papyrussammlung, Schlossstrasse 70, 14059 Berlin and Bodestrasse 1–3, 10178 Berlin; Sammlung des Ägyptologischen Instituts, Universität Heidelberg, Marstallhof 4, 69117 Heidelberg.
Netherlands: Stichting Rijksmuseum van Oudheden, Rapenburg 28, 2311 EW Leiden.

Glossary

Major Deities

MODERN/GREEK	EGYPTIAN	DESCRIPTION
Amun	Amun	Chief god of Thebes worshiped at Karnak
Anubis	Anpu	Jackal-headed mortuary god and guide
Apophis	Apep	Monstrous snake of the otherworld, enemy of the sun
Atum	Itemu	Another creator god of Heliopolis, similar to Re
Bast	Bastet	Cat-headed goddess of magic and vengeance
Duamutef	Duamutef	Jackal-headed son of Horus, protects the stomach
Geb	Geb	God of earth, paired with Nuit
Hapy	Hapy	Baboon-headed son of Horus, protects the lungs
Hathor	Het-Heru	Cow-headed goddess of love and beauty
Heka	Heka	God of magic (feminine form is Weret Hekat)
Heket	Heket	Goddess of midwifery, symbolized by a frog
Horus	Her	Sun king, hero
Horus-Sopedu	Her-Sopedu	Star of the east, son of Horus and Sopdet
Ihy	Ihy	God of music and dance, son of Hathor
Imhotep	Imhotep	Deified mortal, wise sage, god of healing
Imsety	Imsety	Human-headed son of Horus, protects the liver
Isis	Aset	Divine mother and wife, mistress of magic
Khephera	Khepri	Cosmic scarab beetle representing dynamic potential
Khnum	Khnum	Ram-headed potter god, created mankind
Maat	Maat	Goddess of balance, justice, truth, harmony
Nepthys	Nebet-het	Nature goddess, wife of Set
Nuit	Nut	Sky goddess, mother of the gods
Osiris	Wasar	Lord of death and resurrection, corn king
Ptah	Ptah	Creator god of Memphis, god of crafts
Qebensenef	Qebehsenuef	Hawk-headed son of Horus, protects the intestines
Ra	Re	Sun, creator god of Heliopolis, chief of the gods
Re-Harakhti	Re-Harakhti	Horus of the horizon—a manifestation of Re
Sekhmet	Sekhet	Lioness, burning rays of the sun, vengeance, healing
Selkis	Serket	Scorpion goddess, healing goddess
Set (Seth)	Sutekh	Chaos, destruction, violence, storm
Shu	Shu	Element of air, supports the sky goddess
Sothis/Sirus	Sopdet	Star Sirius (dog star) seen as a goddess; heralds the arrival of the Nile flood; equated with Isis
Tefnut	Tefnut	Element of water, moisture (female)
Thoth	Djheuty, Tahuti	Ibis-headed god of medicine, science, arts, magic
Wadjet	Wadjet	Cobra-headed goddess, protector of the pharaoh

Akh The spiritual essence of a dead person.

akhet The time of the Nile inundation, the first season of the Egyptian year.

Amenti The Land of the Dead, ruled over by the risen Osiris.

ankh Hieroglyph for "life," used to represent life beyond death.

BCE Before Common Era.

Book of the Dead *see* Pyramid Texts.

canopic jars Four jars associated with the four sons of Horus in which the vital organs of a mummy were stored. The human-headed Imsety guarded the liver, the baboon Hapy guarded the lungs, the jackal Duamutef guarded the stomach, and the hawk Qebehsenuef the intestines.

CE Common Era.

Coffin Texts *see* Pyramid Texts.

determinative Symbol that indicates a word's meaning.

Djed A symbolic pillar, the backbone of Osiris.

Duat The watery otherworld into which the sun sank in the evening and traveled through during the night to reappear in the morning.

dynasty A series of rulers often from the same line of descent.

Ennead From the Greek word for "nine," a group of nine deities.

Eye of Horus Worn as a protective amulet.

hieroglyphs Pictorial writing of the Egyptians.

hieratic A simplified form of hieroglyphs used for speed.

hypostyle halls A columned hall; feature of Egyptian temples.

Hu The original word of power that created the universe: in Greek, the Logos; translated into English as "Word."

ideogram A symbol that represents an idea or concept.

Ka The vital essence of a human body; the etheric body. The Ka is a double of someone; a ghost.

mummy Based on the Arab word *mummiya*, a type of bitumen. Mummies were the embalmed corpses of the Egyptian dead.

natron Sodium carbonate and bicarbonate used for washing and to preserve mummies.

nome A Greek term for the administrative districts of Egypt.

"Opening of the Mouth" Giving of life to a mummy or statue.

Opet The annual festival held in Thebes in which statues of deities were carried between Karnak and Luxor temples.

papyrus An early form of paper.

pyramid A structure with a square base and four triangular sides meeting at an apex. Used as tombs for early pharaohs.

Pyramid Texts Religious texts inscribed on the walls of the pyramids. They were written originally to protect the spirit of dead pharaohs in the afterlife. Later they became known as the *Book of the Dead*.

rekhet "Knowing One"—term used to describe a female spirit medium.

relief Sculpture chiseled from a flat or curved surface.

scarab A sacred dung beetle, a symbol of the sun. Scarabs were placed near the heart position of mummies.

sistrum A rattle sacred to Hathor and used in temple worship.

stele Wood or stone carved or painted with scenes or texts.

Udjat or Wedjat *see* Eye of Horus.

Wadjet or Edjo The cobra-headed goddess of Lower Egypt who protects the pharaoh.

Ushabti or Shabti A servant in the afterlife.

Index

A

afterlife 22
alphabet 70–1
amulets 44–53
   consecrating 50–3
   magical protection 45
   symbols, types of 46–8
Anubis 92, 98
appearance 20–1
archeoastronomy 57
art 24–6
astrology 55–67

B

Ba 56–7
Bakir, Dr Abd El-Mohsen 62
Book of the Dead 68, 111

C

Cairo Calendar 62–3
calendar 55, 62–3
chants 76–9
   Amun-Re 76–7
   healing 122
charms 83–7
childbirth 16
childhood 17–19
courtship 82

D

dawn ceremony 78–9
dead
   offerings to 75
   petitioning 74
deities 30–7
distance healing 121
divination 92–6
doctors 109
dreams 96–9

E

education 18
exercises 8
   amulet, consecration 50–3
   glamor rite 86–7
   good fortune ritual 64–7
   healing ceremony 122–3
   Isis image 25–6
   meditation on Isis 38–41
   Osiris, calling to 57
   scrying 94–6

F

farming 12–13
feathers, symbolism 72–3
floods 13

G

glamor rite 86–7
grain 13

H

Harris Papyrus 82
Hathor 84–7
healing
   ceremony 122
   combined 120–1
   deities 116–8
   herbal 114–5
   spells 111
   spiritual 112–3
Heka 42
Hermapolis Magna 119
hieroglyphs 69–73
Horus 34–5, 37
   eye of 49
   Hathor, links with 84–5

I

Imhotep 96, 119
Isis
   drawing an image of 25–6
   Fellowship of 9, 125
   meditation on 38–41

K

Ka 56–7

L

language 69–77
life after death 22
literature 81
lotus flower 115
love 83–7
lucky and unlucky days 62–3

M

Maat 29
magical protection 45

N

Narmer 12
Nile and Delta 11

O

old age 23
"Opening the Mouth" 89
oracles 89–92
Osiris 34–5, 57

P

papyrus 69
pharaoh 14–15
prayers to deities 78–9
pyramids 15, 57–9

R

racial characteristics 20–1
Re 36, 78–9
rekhet 89
rites of passage 17
ritual for good fortune 64–7
Rosetta Stone 72
Royal Family *see* pharaoh

S

saluting the sun 78
sanctifying your sacred space 104–5
scrying 92–6
Sekhmet 113
Selket 116
Sirius, rising of 56
society 14–19
spells 73, 83–7, 111
spirituality 9–10
Sun Gods 36–7
swnw ("soo-noo") 109
sympathetic magic 44

T

talismans 83–7
Thoth 116–9
toys 19
Tutmosis, Prince 97

U

Ushabti 101
   awakening 106–7
   making an 102–3
   using 107

Z

Zodiac, Denderah 61